I0821578

Published by
Evolo Press
6363 Wilshire Blvd, 311
Los Angeles CA, 90048

visit our website at: www.evolo.us

Printed and Bound in the United States of America
First Edition

Front cover image
2018 Casey Rehm

Back cover image
2018 Casey Rehm

Editor: Carlo Aiello
Designer: Jose Sanchez

BLINDSPOT INITIATIVE:
DESIGN RESISTANCE AND ALTERNATIVE MODES OF PRACTICE

Jose Sanchez

ACKNOWLEDGMENTS

Kickstarter Supporters:

Erin Reynolds, Samantha G., Gabriel Morales-Olivares, Nels Long, Sydney Brown, Alexander Sheft, Jakub Galczynski, Ján Pernecký, Brian Harms, John Hupp, Victoria Dam, Akif Yagiz Saraclar, Jacob Narvaez, Abdi Ahsan, Ryan Goulden, ttaa:lab, Beau Lawrence, Marilyn Creswell, FRM, Amy Murphy, Daniel Christopher, Federico Borello, Rodrigo Shiordia Lopez, Lauren Diaz, Hameleon-ed, Larry Hays, Milena, Léopold Lambert, Dianab, Johnny Martinez, Gilles Retsin, Alessio Erioli, Stephen Hartounian, Henry Cheung, Kelsi Goss, Alicia Nahmad, Ezio Blasetti, Edward Luckmann, Denis Lacej, Igor Pantic, Arthur Carabott, Rene Peralta, Knut Brunier, Robbie Eleazer, Elizabeth Leidy, Chia-ching Yang, Jen Stein, Yolanda Recio Martínez, Luis Quinones, Emmanuelle Chiappone-Piriou, Gregory Zamora, Synthesis DnA, Jonathan Pickett, Natalie Popik, Jana Baumann, Richie Bisso, Sasha Bell, Melanie Mandl, Manuel Jimenez Garcia, Rob Ley, Armin J Bogosian, Alan J Bergman, Mataillet Yannis, Aaron Whelton, Nikita Troufanov, Cheng, Alec Chiu, Edward Jahangir, Joseph Sarafian, Andrew E. M. Graham, Oli Tirado, Matthew Gehm, Zachary Matthews, Abeer Basha, Bryan Dimagiba, Luis Dimagiba, Tingting Xu, Lorik Khodaverdian, Nicole Koltick, Andrew Lau, Eugene Lee, Ping-Hsiang Chen, Golnaz Ebrahimi, Jorge Ramirez, Carlos Perez, Jordan Perkins, Sherif Tarabishy, bb, Mark Guerrero, Arthur Mamou-Mani, Jack Love, María Graciela Sánchez, Xavier Schrader, Pedro Orueta, George Tsakiridis, Mariannah Amster, Meropi Karantaki, Vasiliki Diamanti, Angelopoulou Dimitra, Tommy Frauenfelder, Ying Xiao, Daniel Widrig, Christos Sazos, Alexa Roman, Massimiliano Manno, Efthymia Dimitra Kotsani, Elvira Perfetto & Omrana Ahmed.

This book has been made possible by the collaborative effort of many individuals over the course of three years. The project begins as a Kickstarter campaign in March 2014, in which the designers who featured in the exhibition offered technical workshops in exchange for funding to make the exhibition and publication possible. After successfully reaching our goal, we curated an exhibition at Keystone Gallery, in Los Angeles, featuring new work from 10 young architects and designers. We are very grateful to all the Kickstarter supporters, and to Keystone Gallery, to make this possible.

I would specifically like to acknowledge the contribution and hard work the following individuals:

-Participants of the Blindspot exhibition: Biayna Bogosian, Jason King, Sacha Baumann, Luis Quinones, Nicholas Hanna, Catherine Griffiths, Satoru Sugihara, Michael Kontopoulos, Zach Schoch and Myles Sciotto.

-Evolo and Carlo Aiello for supporting this publication to become more ambitious and helping to structure the content more explicitly.

-My co-curators and co-organizers of the Blindspot exhibition and campaign, Biayna Bogosian, Jason King and Sacha Baumann, who played a central and critical role in making the Blindspot Initiative happen.

-Rebekah Bukhbinder and Gentaro Makinoda who worked on the design of this publication, and Catherine Griffiths who continuously supported this project over the past years.

Finally, I feel sincere gratitude to all our Kickstarter supporters, who sponsored this publication and have waited so patiently for a copy of this book.

Jose Sanchez

INDEX

FOREWORD

CASEY REAS

Casey Reas writes software to explore conditional systems as art. Through defining emergent networks and layered instructions, he has defined a unique area of visual experience that builds upon concrete art, conceptual art, experimental animation, and drawing. While dynamic, generative software remains his core medium, work in variable media including prints, objects, installations, and performances materialize from his visual systems.

Reas is a professor at the University of California, Los Angeles. He holds a masters degree from the Massachusetts Institute of Technology in Media Arts and Sciences as well as a bachelors degree from the School of Design, Architecture, Art, and Planning at the University of Cincinnati. With Ben Fry, Reas initiated Processing in 2001. Processing is an open source programming language and environment for the visual arts.

IDEA, PLATFORM, PROCESS, DOMAIN

I make things — all the time. In the studio, I use tools every day. Some of the tools are "hard" like a screwdriver but most of them are "soft." I move back and forth between making software tools, using my tools, and using tools created by others.

I need to have precise control of my tools to form my ideas and I need to be able to modify my tools to explore new ideas. I want to believe that I can form unique ideas, in contrast to accepting the ideas that are encoded into the software tools that I'm using. Through the tools that I make, modify, and use, I sometimes feel like I am in control and sometimes I feel like my ideas are heavily biased by software that others have made. This is the quandary that I'm thinking about today.

IDEA

I have ideas about how software tools can be improved for myself and communities of other creators. I want to be a part of creating a future that I have experienced only in fits and starts in the recent past and present. I have seen independent creators build local and networked communities to share intellectual resources and tools. The individuals in these communities share the responsibility to contribute ideas and infrastructure to making their own tools. It's an aspiration toward a way of making and sharing that has been strongest in one area of the visual arts, the world of creator-programmers. I want to try to scale it within that context and I also want to know if it's applicable to other areas.

The converse to this is more widespread. In this model, creators pay software companies to license the tools that the software company has defined and produced. The essence is paying a company to make decisions about software tools in exchange for not having to conceive one's own tools.

Both of the models described above break down in wide practice and both are ideals from different points of view. One privileges flexibility, freedom, and collective responsibility and the other promises ease of use in exchange for payment. Because neither model works well in the present, I suggest that we should work toward a model that empowers creators to control their own tools.

This isn't an argument for one economic system over another, it's about shared infrastructure for creative work with a collective goal to create flexible tools. It's about empowering people to create through access to tools and platforms. This is also not an argument about dissolving intellectual property and copyrights; it's about finding a balance between shared common infrastructure and individual ownership.

This aspiration is possible through free software where the word free relates to "freedom", not "free lunch" — because we all know there is no such thing. Along with free software, we also need open standards and collective desire to be in control of our platforms and tools.

The contrast to this model is proprietary knowledge and resources. Today, creative communities rely almost exclusively on for-profit corporations to create and control their tools. Companies package what could be modular, general systems into a monolithic, proprietary products. The result is that it's easy to color correct a photograph if you have the financial resources for the product or you are willing to break the law by using a cracked copy, but creative control is stifled when an idea is outside the boundaries of a product that can't be extended or adapted.

So far, this short text has been general and vague, but I want to be specific and clear. As one case study, I will discuss the development of the Processing software that I co-founded in 2001 with Ben Fry. Processing is one example of a free, open, and modular software system with a focus on collaboration and community. It's the example that I know intimately inside and out so I will use it to reflect on the ideas sketched out in the first part of this text.

PLATFORM

The Processing software is an integrated programming language and environment. It's primarily for students and professionals within the visual arts including design, art, and architecture, but it has evolved in time to find a place within the humanities and sciences, even including university computer science programs and high school math and science classes.

From the start, Processing was created as free and open-source software (FOSS) to be accessible and flexible. By access, we mean two things. First, that people can get it; it can be downloaded without cost — it's "free." Second, we mean that it can be understood by a general audience. Processing is simple, but not simplified. We aspire to make the interface easy to use and the documentation clear and free of unnecessary technical jargon.

Ben and I grew up with the first generation of home computers and the culture surrounding them permeated our environments. Computers were simpler then and the code was too. Everything felt possible and we were ready.The hardware and software was designed to be modified and diagrams and code for both were often shared. It was expected that a computer user was also a computer *programmer* — how else would you make the machine do what you wanted it to? If you liked games, you could write your own. If you liked music, you could write a program to help you compose. The computer was an environment for creation and authorship. To reference Howard Rheingold, computers were *Tools for Thought.*

About fifteen years later when we were in our twenties, we experienced and participated in the initial spread of the world wide web. The web extended values from decades prior — it accelerated the promise of more universal access to information, of creating new kinds of communities, and of breaking down hierarchies. These values are shared with the origins of Processing.

As an example, in the first years of the web, many people learned to create web pages by reading sites' HTML directly through the "View Source" feature built into browsers. Inspired by this open quality, the early versions of Processing had an export feature that, by default, included the source code as well as a web-ready files that could be uploaded to a server to share the work with an international audience.

Processing was positioned in a unique space when it was first launched in 2001. It wasn't a tool to make programming easy for visual artists in the tradition of Hypercard and Director. It also wasn't a programming language for professionals in the tradition of C++ and Java. It was a place between, a middle ground where visual artists and designers could be confident with their ability to work with form and images while learning programming and engineers could be confident in their ability to write code while learning about form and images.

It's hard to pin down what Processing is, precisely. I admit, it can be confusing, but here it is: it's both a programming environment and a programming language, but it's also an approach to building a software tool that incorporates its community into the definition. It's more accurate to call Processing a platform — a platform for experimentation, thinking, and learning. It's a foundation and beginning more than a conclusion.

Processing was (and still is) made for sketching and it was created as a space for collaboration. It was born at the MIT Media Lab, a place where C. P. Snow's two cultures (the humanities and the sciences) could synthesize. Processing had the idea to expand this synthesis out of the Lab and into new communities with a focus on access, distribution, and community. Processing is what it is today because of the initial decisions that Ben and I made back in 2001 and the subsequent ways we've listened to the community and incorporated contributions and feedback since the beginning. Processing was inspired by the programming languages BASIC and Logo in general, and specifically by John Maeda's Design By Numbers, C++ code created by the Visual Language Workshop and Aesthetics and Computation Group at the MIT Media Lab, and PostScript. Processing wasn't pulled from the air, it was deeply rooted in decades of prior work.

PROCESS

While Processing started out as the work of two people who volunteered their time, it quickly outgrew what was possible for Ben and I to manage. Increased expectations and ambitions for Processing emerged when other people started to use it. Early on, we needed to do two things. First, to figure out how to collaborate with other people and second, how to remove ourselves as bottlenecks to moving forward.

For collaboration, we found amazing people through the internet who were excited to volunteer time to work with us on certain aspects of the project. However, we weren't able to find help for some of the more technically difficult under-the-hood programming tasks. So from early on, we've needed to secure some funding for the project to hire out some pieces of the code in balance with working closely with volunteers. As some collaborators contributed more to the work, they organically moved closer to the center and into more specific roles within the project. Over time, Florian Jenett, Andreas Schlegel, Elie Zananiri, Andres Colubri, Dan Shiffman, and Scott Murray became essential. Dan became a third official project lead when we started the Processing Foundation in 2012. Many, many other volunteers made crucial contributions over the years — too many to list here, but it's all archived at www.processing.org.

In addition, Ben and I were spending our evenings and weekends working on the project and that has largely continued into the present, but we now require more balance. Like our collaborators, we now have even more challenging responsibilities outside of working on Processing. That brings us to the second point, the need to remove the core team as bottlenecks to the growth of the project.

This is done through more shared responsibility and developing the software in a modular way. The goal for Processing has always been to have a minimal code base and interface. It's a different type of software development than a program that is sold and marketed based on new features that are continuously added and removed to encourage or force upgrades. Processing has a core that changes slowly, while the structure of the code supports libraries to extend the software quickly into new areas.

A Processing library is a standalone piece of code that integrates into the core to extend what is possible. With only a few exceptions, libraries are contributed by the community of people who use Processing. The generous developers who make and share libraries document their open code as well as host the files for download. More than anything, libraries have allowed Processing to expand into unexpected directions and they are a remarkable example of a community of individuals sharing responsibility for building and maintaining a free software infrastructure.

As a free software project, Processing utilizes other free software projects. Processing was built by combining modular pieces of free software together and adding more code to create a new coherent whole. If the entire project was written from scratch, it would have required a team of engineers and more time. We had neither.

It's also important to say that we didn't want to raise money to write Processing from scratch and we didn't want to work on Processing full time or to manage a team of people to work on Processing full time. We made Processing to help us with our primary work. In Ben's case, this was creating visualizations for the Human Genome Project and in my case, to teach designers the basics of computer programing and to explore code in my visual arts practice. We needed a tool to support the work we did — to develop ideas and forms in our own context. We had (and still have) no interest in working full time to make a tool.

Our system of guidelines and relationships that enabled the software to be maintained and to improve broke down slowly and reached a critical point around the time of the Processing 2.0 release. The expectations of the community and the complexity of the software had grown to a point where volunteered "free time" of the core developers and occasional help could not complete the work without deep personal sacrifices. To attempt to keep the project moving, we started the Processing Foundation as a legal not-for-profit 501(c)(3) organization. We started to ask for donations from the community at the time the software is downloaded. The truth is that we need substantial funding to keep the software maintained and improving and the ideal of a 100% volunteer effort coordinated through the internet wasn't working for our specific situation. We finally acknowledged that free software is expensive to make.

Processing evolved through building on top of existing tools and collaborating with others to share the responsibility. That is still the case today, but the development is also supplemented through donations from the community, programs like Google's Summer of Code, and occasional generosity from academic institutions (New York University, Miami University, University of Denver), companies (O'Reilly), and other open-source projects that use our code (Arduino).

On the tenth anniversary of the Processing software in 2011, we made a list of what we felt was essential to the project:

• Programming in an art context
• Straightforward but not simplified, scale complexity
• Made for education and learning
• Bridge to other languages and platforms
• Provide infrastructure for learning and teaching
• Develop through teaching
• Simple publishing for sharing
• Community infrastructure
• Extensible through libraries
• Import/export To diverse media and formats

In 2015, I re-assessed this list and synthesized it to this core:

- Access
- Community
- Free (Libre, Libero)

I feel that with more detail (as I have started to flesh out above), these three points are the core of Processing and they differentiate its approach from proprietary, consumer-driven software.

DOMAIN

These core ideas outlined in this text emerged within the culture of free software. Free software is primarily created by technical folks for other technical folks — it has been most successful in the realm of systems administration and operating systems in projects like the Apache Web Server and GNU/Linux. The Free Software Foundation and its "copyleft" idea has been the pioneer and uncompromising proponent that "any user can study the source code, modify it, and share the program."

Artists have also pioneered new ideas about intellectual property. For instance, the first Radical Software publication in 1970 introduced an anti-copyright symbol, an "x" within a circle to mean "DO copy." Dan Sandin introduced his Distribution Religion in the early 1970s so the schematics for his Image Processor could be "copied by individuals and not-for-profit institutions without charge."

Ideas about free access to information are less tested in areas of the arts that have more physical outcomes, that is architecture, sculpture, product design, fashion design, jewelry, ceramics, etc. There have been explorations for many years, but these tests have yet to fundamentally transform these areas. The software used within these fields can follow existing models, but what about the "hard" tools, the more material technologies?
These approaches are less tested in areas of the visual arts that have more tangible outcomes, meaning architecture, sculpture, product design, fashion design, jewelry, ceramics, etc. Can the ideas outlined here apply to these areas? They certainly can for the software used within these fields, but what about the "hard" tools, the more real technologies?

The technologies that may enable this transition are newer than those required for free software. They have developed rapidly within the last decade and to a large extent they are still nascent. New types of computer-controlled fabrication technologies and new cultures emerging around crowdfunding might be a strong foundation for new opportunities.

Through initiatives like Processing, communities of creators are working to realize a new vision for software and fabrication within the arts with the goal of controlling of our own tools. In time, will this grow or diminish? Is this a trend or is it more substantial? The model of our communities paying a company for licenses to use standardized software that will "just work" is a model that might make sense in the category of functional productivity software, but has little relevance to artists and designers who thrive on radical exploration. I want to succeed in pursuing this new path; I want you to succeed; I think it's important and it can be done.

INTRODUCTION

JOSE SANCHEZ

Jose Sanchez is an Architect / Game Developer based in Los Angeles, California. He is a partner at Bloom Games, start-up built upon the BLOOM project, winner of the WONDER SERIES hosted by the City of London for the London 2012 Olympics. He is the director of the Plethora Project, a research and learning project investing in the future of online open-source knowledge He is also the creator of Block'hood, a city simulator video game exploring notions of crowdsourced urbanism named by the Guardian one of the most anticipated games of 2016.

He has taught and guest lectured in several renowned institutions across the world, including the Architectural Association in London, the University of Applied Arts in Vienna, ETH Zurich, The Bartlett School of Architecture, University College London.

Today, he is an Assistant Professor at USC School of Architecture in Los Angeles. His research 'Gamescapes', explores generative interfaces in the form of video games, speculating in modes of intelligence augmentation, combinatorics, and open systems as a design medium.

DESIGN RESISTANCE & ALTERNATIVES MODES OF PRACTICE

Competitions have become a fundamental mechanism by which an architectural design commission is allocated to a design firm. It is a means of crowdsourcing the best design idea from thousands of designs, allowing the winner to take all. In principle, this may sound fair, but when we look more closely into the culture this promotes, we unveil a culture of exploitation and undervaluing of labor, where many small players absorb all the risks. This kind of strategy could be more understandable if a computer performed it, where thousands of permutations are calculated and discarded to generate an optimum design solution. However, the same process becomes problematic when described as follows: a large group of individuals performs free labor to generate a myriad of ideas and solutions that will be discarded at the end of the process without any remuneration. Even worst, many competitions will charge a fee to participate.

When we look at design competitions, we focus on the winner and a few more notably radical proposals that emerge from the model. In 2015, Harvard Graduate School of Design hosted the 'Design Competitions' conference, in which Mohsen Mostafavi, in his opening keynote presentation[1] discussed the notion of gifts in architecture, by recalling the significant achievements in competitions in recent history. It seems ingrained in our architectural and design culture to accept this notion of the gift as a symbol of the passion and dedication that our profession has for the discipline, which often justifies long working hours and poor working conditions that many, especially young, architects endure in order to have a chance to become part of a good design firm.

Daniel Dendra, in his talk at TedxBerlin in 2007[2], explains how the nature of competitions generates lost labor. He calculated that an average of 4671 architects distributed over 1557 design firms invested in designing proposals for the Grand Egyptian Museum of Cairo competition, some hours that is equivalent to the lifetimes work of ten architects. This demonstrates a profoundly unsustainable practice, where unpaid and poorly paid jobs, including internships, propel an idealism that mostly serves the client and the architectural firms that have already won the jackpot and been elevated to stardom as a consequence of sheer improbability. The business model for this type of practice revolves around increasing the odds of winning a competition through an accumulation of fast proposals, knowing that the unpredictable nature of competitions is high, and no competition is worth developing an idea in great depth. This is how specialized competition teams are assembled within architecture firms, that jump from one competition to the next to maximize the chances of striking a chord with the jury. The consequences of this practice are exploitative: the fostering of a business model that is based on unpaid and poorly paid workers (how else could firms enter competitions with such unlikely odds of seeing a return on investment); and also a poor model of research, which does not promote the accumulation of knowledge and excellence. In fact, most competitions promote secrecy among participants, by not encouraging the orchestrated crowd operation to benefit from any collective knowledge. The possibility of collective thinking over a given design problem is a fallacy that serves the organizers and clients. This is how competitions devalue design by making it become a nearly free commodity. Competitions serve

Fig. 1.1 Guggenheim Competition entries, 1715 entries.

the purpose of concentrating capital, polarizing design practice, and devaluing the immaterial labor that is inherited to architectural design.

The problems that competitions present cannot be resolved by competitions themselves; instead they need to be addressed by alternative modes of practice that can grow and enrich the discipline.
In 2015, the Guggenheim Foundation held one of the largest design competitions to date for the new Guggenheim Helsinki and received 1,715 submissions[3]. Collectively, these submissions have been estimated to represent over 18,000,000 Euros of free work. Not without its controversies, the Guggenheim Foundation awarded the price to Moreau Kusunoki Architects. The Guggenheim Foundation tried to offset controversy by running a fully transparent process, by documenting all of the submissions, in an attempt to convey the idea that each participant was part of a broader conversation around the innovation of architecture for such an iconic building. This transparency worked as a branding mechanism, but it did not serve the purpose innovation through collective thinking; the website only revealed all of the design proposals when the competition had ended, so any possibility of collective knowledge became a retroactive practice, which is a weak model of knowledge propagation. In no way was a crowd-sourced operation encouraged in the development of a collective voice that could be in dialogue with the client.

There is a noticeable development in the discussion around design competitions, where other disciplines are also starting to face the issues that architects have been dealing with as the status quo. In 2011, the Huffington Post received strong criticism when they launched a design competition inviting their audience to redesign the brand's logo[4]. The criticism led to the anti-spec and No!Spec movements, which advocate against the practice of speculative work. Speculative work in this context is defined by work that requires either a large number of people to develop ideas for free from which only one person will be paid, or a single individual to develop ideas for free, where perhaps one, or sometimes none at all, will be selected as a paid commission. The main criticism from the anti-spec movement is the expectation of free labor and the devaluation of the design discipline. The fact that speculative work and competitions are so prevalent in

the field of design is evidence of how we value our discipline in general.
With the increase of digital technologies, there is increasing use of crowdsourcing as a technique for community engagement, and it has become cleverly utilized by corporations for branding and public outreach. Speculative work, especially the contest or competition model, sit at the center of this discussion. In his book, Digital Labor: The internet as playground and factory, Trebor Scholz curates a series of essays that discuss the current state and problems with labor in the digital era[5]. In his essay titled In search of the lost paycheck, Andrew Ross explains:
"free, or token-wage, labor is increasingly available through a variety of channels: crowdsourcing; data mining or other sophisticated digital techniques for extracting rents from users/participants; expanded prison labor programs; the explosion of unpaid, near-obligatory internships in every white-collar sector; and the whole gamut of contestant volunteering that has transformed so much of our commerce in culture into an amateur talent show, with jackpot stakes for a few winners and hard-luck swag for everyone else" [6]

In his analysis of the work of Ross Perlin [7], he continues:
"The biggest beneficiary of this galloping trade, of course, is the employer. In Ross Perlin's book on the internship explosion, he estimates that corporate America enjoys a $2 billion annual subsidy from internships alone, and this sum does not include the massive tax dodges that many firms execute through employer misclassification, (...) An estimated 50% of U.S. internships are now unpaid or below minimum wage, 51% in Germany, and 37% in the United Kingdom."

This practice has long lived within architectural and design culture, and it's only going to increase with the proliferation of platforms such as 99 Designs [8] and Amazon's Mechanical Turk, which allow anyone to create a commission to which an unlimited number of workers give free labor in the hope of becoming the sole winner. Taking a typical commission on 99 Designs, Scholz [9] calculates that as an example, a $300 commission will result in the winner receiving $180 for their design chosen from a pool of approximately 116 fully executed design proposals, with the remaining $120 going to the intermediary, in this case, 99 Designs. Examples such as these insist on the devaluation of design, promoting an asymmetrical power relation between client and designer. Under the competition model or the new crowdsourcing platforms, it is becoming rarer to see clients who appreciate the design discipline and are willing to risk giving agency to a professional designer. It could be argued that the Guggenheim Foundation has been such a client in the past, when they chose Frank Gehry to design the Guggenheim Museum in Bilbao for example, however, they have now switched to a competition model which signifies a step away from the acknowledgment of the architect's agency, and toward the requirement that a large number of proposals must be generated before a commission can be made.

Ayhan Aytes denounces the way that crowdsourcing has become a significant element of a neoliberal economy where immaterial labor plays a structural role[10]. He describes crowdsourcing as a hybrid concept that merges the neoliberal outsourcing paradigm with the availability of crowds on digital networks.
"In digital labor markets maintained by crowdsourcing protocols, crowds are subjected to a form of division of labor that is reminiscent of industrial production. However, the division of labor differs from the industrial division of labor regarding its effect in its relation to the global neoliberal socioeconomic formations that constitute

Fig. 1.2 "The Johnny Cash Project" by Aaron Koblin & Chris Milk

a distinct condition for the workers of the global south. These conditions could be described as the gray zones of international laws that are designed by neoliberal policies to take advantage of stark regional differences in labor costs, which Ailwa Ong[11] conceptualizes as "system of exceptions."[12]

While Aytes considers crowdsourcing an apparatus of a neoliberal system of exception, not all crowdsourcing seeks the convergence of value for neoliberal agendas. We can also find examples where the opposite happens; the use of crowdsourcing as an apparatus for collective intelligence, one that can distribute and propagate value among the members of the network.

ETHICAL CROWDSOURCING

Crowdsourcing cannot be only generalized as a neoliberal strategy as the nuances of its setup can yield essential variations in the distribution of value. In the most straightforward sense, crowdsourcing can be organized towards competition as we have examined, but it can also be used towards cooperation. With the right motivation, crowdsourcing can become a meaningful way for public engagement and participation, one in which any individual that participates could learn and obtain value from a collective enterprise. The artist, Aaron Koblin, has discussed the need to avoid crowdsourcing as a competition model and find mechanisms to foster cooperation. His video The Johnny Cash Project, 2010, in collaboration with Chris Milk[13], Koblin explores the use of crowd collaboration by inviting an online audience to each contribute a drawing of Johnny Cash that becomes a frame of the final video. By providing the participants with some intuitive digital painting tools and alienating them from the collective outcome, each participant was able to contribute a unique frame which reflected their sentiment toward the artist and his work.

The key in Koblin's piece comes at the moment of combining these individual frames to construct the final video, using the creations of thousands of participants. The issue with this strategy is one of aggregation and collective participation, where the freely contributed labor by each participant is part of the final more significant output and one that is specifically meaningful to all those who participated. The key point here is that the collective result is of value to each participant, rather than being an anonymous cloud worker. This is a case where 'winner does not take all', but rather the construction is the added value of the collective.

This form of crowdsourcing can be seen at play in the open source community. The work of any individual contributing to any open source project is of value to both the broader enterprise and to the individual. Free labor is compensated from a network of knowledge and incentives to challenge and share ideas. The ethos of many open source projects is that of collaboration and free access to knowledge, understanding that the only way to move forward is by a promiscuous propagation of ideas.

Open source also offers the possibility to maintain a notion of authorship, where not all the work goes into a general project, but preferably we have visibility of authored chapters that can work together. Processing[14] is an open source software and programming platform, developed by Casey Reas and Ben Fry in 2001. The project was inspired by John Maeda's Design By Numbers and quickly started gathering users worldwide. Processing reduced the friction for learning how to program by hiding some of the advanced features of the Java language. One of the critical ideas behind Processing (and of programming in general) is the possibility to grow the software and its capabilities. Processing will ship with functions developed by the core Processing team, but anyone can develop libraries and share new features for the project. A processing library is an open source module authored for a specific purpose. The author of such a module is credited for their contribution and is connected to a larger collaborative environment. As the libraries themselves must also be open source, anyone is free to look into the code and learn and expand its functionalities further. This was an ethos at the heart of the Processing project, and this open source mentality and community approach are expressed and propagated on its website. As a result of this, the free collaborative effort of thousands of individuals has allowed Processing to grow and become one of the primary platforms for prototyping software today in the field of design. Processing crosses disciplines, having been developed without a precise agenda, which enables the platform to be free to evolve and adapt to the requirements of its users.

Jeremy Rifkin, writing in The Zero Marginal Cost Society, explains how open source strategies, which until this day have been most common among software development, are starting to transition towards the production of physical goods. "The hackers immediately realized the potential of conceiving of "atoms as the new bits." These pioneers envisioned bringing the open-source format from the Internet of Things and computing arena into the production of "things." Open-source hardware became the rallying cry of a disperse group of inventors and enthusiasts loosely identifying themselves as part of the Maker Movement." [15]

For Rifkin, the emergence of collaborative networks is an indication of a new economic system that could challenge the capitalist status quo:

"Lost in all of the excitement over the prospect of the Internet of Things is that connecting everyone and everything in a global network driven by extreme productivity moves us ever faster towards an era of nearly free goods and services and, with it, the shrinking of capitalism in the next half of the century and the rise of the Collaborative Commons as the dominant model of organizing economic life." [16]

For this to effectively be the case, we need to celebrate modes of practice that move away from the neoliberal exploitation of networks and resist the emerging models of crowdsourcing and speculative work for our design field. Some may argue that professional associations or legislation should address this matter, but there is no stronger message than the proliferation of alternative modes of practice, paths that encourage individuals to cooperate and resist neoliberal agendas.

THE SELF COMMISSION

Many young architects, designers, and firms decide to enter competitions to develop their skills for larger architectural projects and to develop a portfolio of work to enable opportunities in the future, however, the research conducted for any given competition entry can rarely be developed in depth, as competition deadlines are typically three to four months. Most of that time will not be dedicated to the generation of new knowledge but rather to the execution of a design problem with the tools that a team already has. Research, on the other hand, is work that requires more time to develop to explore how a topic could work and cannot be bound by a tight deadline, especially the expectation of a working solution in such a timeframe.

Other fields, such as computer science, have developed a culture that has been popularized as the 'garage culture' where a group of engineers or designers embark on an entrepreneurial project to develop their ideas and drive them into the market. It is a high-risk strategy, but one in which the free labor of a team is in the longer-term interests of the team and the development of their capital. Many of these practitioners focus on ideas of intellectual property (IP) to quantify the value of the labor and would not consider giving that away without proper remuneration. One could argue that this is a more radical approach, as the ideas of different teams have the potential to be more disruptive and fundamentally redefine the discipline in which they were conceived. Such ideas have the power to blur the boundaries of the discipline that conceived them and fundamentally challenge the status quo of the field.

However, here we must confront a paradox; while entrepreneurialism can be seen as a step towards autonomy for a labor force of young architects that have been subjugated by the competition apparatus, the result of such a move will displace architects deeper into capitalism's notion of freedom, one in which the creative entrepreneur is bound by market pressures or media attention. As Peggy Deamer reminds us in her reading of David Harvey,

"The neo-liberal agenda can best be advanced by liberating individual entrepreneurial freedoms and skills within and skills within an institutional framework characterized by strong private property rights, free markets, and free trade." [17]

Still, this first move is necessary as it provides the first order of autonomy in the tradition of practice; it reallocates value to the labor and craftsmanship of designers and attempts to get rid of architectural aggregators that through armies of unpaid professionals, privileged networks, and intense media presence, can create brands that exploit actual merit.

We can detect three tiers in the capitalist model that would organize workers in the diagram below.

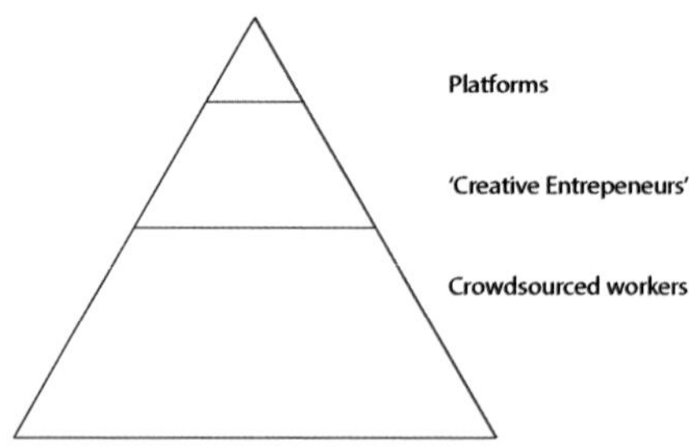

In the bottom of the pyramid, we have all the workers that provide free or unfairly paid content to aggregators or platforms. This group is often unconcerned with intellectual property or believe they just need to get some more experience to break into the market. On the second tier, we can detect the creative entrepreneur, who is aware of the value proposition of immaterial labor, and often uses mechanisms like intellectual property or copyrights to protect their rights and produce value from immaterial labor. While some members of this group are ok with maintaining this status, some will attempt to move up the pyramid and become platforms. The top 1% of the pyramid are platform aggregators; entities which produce little content but can orchestrate a community to provide work, (hopefully for free) to expand a brand. Architecture as a field has yet to see the rise of platforms like YouTube or Uber that can profit by merely orchestrating the needs of design with designers that can provide the service. Competitions, on a smaller scale, are micro platform operations that use the model described above for generating a significant amount of value at an incredibly low cost.

It is time for architecture, as other disciplines have already begun, to address the unethical practices that this model entails.

TOWARDS COLLECTIVISM

The pyramid model described above presents the structure that many other disciplines have adopted in embracing the model of platform capitalism that seems to be the state of affairs at the beginning of the 21st century, and while architecture has been late to the party, perhaps that lag can be transformed into a critical reflection for the construction of an alternative.

If the first move of resistance is a critical assessment of the mechanisms that provide working opportunities and a creative approach needed to generate them, a final goal should become a collective project that can continue beyond any individual success, challenging the concept of the star architect that has been an outcome, perhaps an optimum of the current system. This book is an attempt to contribute to such a collective project, increasing the threads that connect expert lines of research. An awareness of practices that live in the blind spots of each project.

It is with these ideas in mind that this publication emerged, to highlight the work being developed by independent designers and small firms that work outside of the competition paradigm. We specifically sought out work that connected personal lines of research and that in different areas, questions and expands the field of design and architecture into new hybrids across different domains.

This publication emerged as a form of design resistance to the competition model, by evaluating the viability of alternative modes of practice, already present in our discipline. In many cases, architects and designers are required to leave their field or hybridize their knowledge to push for innovation. While competitions are often marketed under a call for radical innovation and design difference, the results rarely escape a predicted outcome specified by the brief. In this sense, they have become a mechanism for the preservation of a power relationship between clients and architects.

THE INITIATIVE

The 'Blindspot Initiative' was the result of a collaboration between Jason King, Biayna Bogosian, Sacha Baumann, and Jose Sanchez to explore the space of self-financing and self-commissioning new work. From the critique of competitions, the 'Blindspot Initiative' attempted to create a different loop between design and resources. The hypothesis goes as follows:

-The creation of new work produces new knowledge.

-That knowledge has value if it is documented and propagated.

-The new creative work could be sustained by the value of the knowledge necessary to create it.

Out of this premise, we embarked on a

Kickstarter campaign to enable the team to set up the framework for our self-imposed commission, one in which any supporter could benefit from the outcome, by obtaining this publication, by participating in workshops or talks or just by attending the exhibition. This model does not result in 99% of the losing side obtaining no value from taking part in the enterprise. On the contrary, the initiative attempts to benefit designers and supporters by committing to sharing and propagating the ideas developed in work. While the exhibition only allowed us to work with designers based in Los Angeles, the publication allowed us to reach out and engage with a generation of designers propelled by their ideas and skills.

This book is divided into five chapters. Each chapter explores how a particular industry has influenced both the process and outcome of a group of designers' work. For each chapter, we have an opening article followed by a selection of work by designers working within that domain.

Chapter 1 explores the work of material research and physical prototyping. Design is not always developed towards a specific application, and designers find it useful to explore material concepts that could be exhibited, allowing them to generate small commissions and slowly grow in scale. In retrospect, many architects begin in this way: finding opportunities to present the development of a thought process and its material implications. Here the self-commission is very important, as galleries often don't commission new work, but instead look for completed work from artists or designers. It is in the hands of the designer to fund-raise or seeks sponsorship. Today, many companies find it useful to sponsor young designers to support the design field, and because it is in their interests to be associated with innovation and the arts.

Chapter 2 explores the productive incursions of architects in the field of product design and wearables, exploring on a much smaller scale, the means to drive design innovation and also develop a business model that can stand on its own. While the difficulties of such discipline are new to the architecture field, the continuous proliferation of architects crossing into this field demonstrates that there is something to be learned from a more product-centric, smaller-scale approach. Product design presents all the challenges for a creative entrepreneur and situates the design of the object as one of many items to be addressed to reach the market. In such a field, the means of production and distribution play an important role in success, as well as marketing, and placement.

Chapter 3 seeks to document work that has been influenced by film and new media. The work is screen-based but assumes its medium to raise questions and provide novel perspectives. The cinematic perspective is often focused and intentional becoming an excellent medium for narrative and empathy toward more significant topics. Without the necessity of a built output, new media can speculate on the impact of the digital, ranging from perception to the transaction of actors in a network. The work can visualize processes that are often invisible, happening in the background of our daily life or project on the trajectories that technology is taking. There have been many architects and designers who have crossed into film either by inspiration or as a more powerful storytelling medium, but the questions that film proposes to architecture and design are infused with a novel perspective that supports innovation.

Chapter 4 looks at software as a format and medium for design and architectural thinking. The work in this area often attempts to facilitate the work of others, and it is also a proven alternative business model and research platform that can bring fresh questions to the field of architecture and design. The challenges in this area have to do with the cross-disciplinary skills involved in software development, the creation of development teams with different areas of expertise, and the management of a product that is scalable and can be developed over an extended period. While there are small software ventures, we are seeing designers become more and more ambitious with the scope of their applications, proposing real value to the market.

Chapter 5 looks at how robotics and interactive installations have added a new dimension to the physical world by allowing a dialogue between the physical and the digital. Such work blurs disciplinary boundaries, mixing technical expertise with expression and design intention. Designers cannot just invent new ideas but instead need to think through making; by fabricating prototypes and designing behaviors, new alternatives emerge. One of the most difficult things to forecast is the response of a human towards a new interactive system, and only through iterative prototyping and installations, we can develop the knowledge to make this work meaningful.

Looking beyond work that was initiated by a competition paradigm, the five chapters of this book demonstrate several parallel tracks for creative thinking. This book envisions the propagation of this design ethos in the future, where institutions will not only prepare designers tor studios or competition attempts but also to design new forms of labor and their role into the economy.

[1] Harvard GSD. 2015. "The Design Competition Conference." http://www.gsd.harvard.edu/#/events/the-design-competition-conference.html.

[2] Dendra, Daniel. 2007. "Open Sim-Sim." http://tedxtalks.ted.com/video/TEDxBerlin-Daniel-Dendra-Open-S.

[3] Foundation, Solomon R. Guggenheim. 2014. "Guggenheim Helsinki Design Competition." http://designguggenheimhelsinki.org/.

[4] Byers, Dylan. 2011. "Design Community Up in Arms Over Huffington Post Logo Contest." http://www.adweek.com/news/press/design-community-arms-over-huffington-post-logo-contest-134140.

[5] Scholz, Trebor. 2012. Digital Labor: The Internet as Playground and Factory. Routledge.

[6] Ross, Andrew. 2013. "In the Search of the Lost Paycheck." In Digital Labor The Internet as Playground and Factory, edited by Trebor Scholz. New York: Routledge.

[7] Perlin, Ross. 2012. Intern Nation: How to Earn Nothing and Learn Little in the Brave New Economy. Verso.

[8] 99 Designs. 2008. "99 Designs." http://99designs.com/.

[9] Scholz, Trebor. 2013. "Digital Labor: New Opportunities, Old Inequalities." Re:publica 2013. https://www.youtube.com/watch?v=52CqKIR0rVM.

[10] Aytes, Ayhan. 2012. "Return to the Crowds." In Digital Labor: The Internet as Playground and Factory. Routledge.

[11] Ong, Aihwa. 2006. Neoliberalism as Exception: Mutations in Citizenship and Sovereignty. Duke University Press Books.

[12] Aytes, Ayhan. 2012. "Return to the Crowds." In Digital Labor: The Internet as Playground and Factory. Routledge.

[13] Milk, Chris, and Aaron Koblin. 2010. "The Johnny Cash Project." http://www.thejohnnycashproject.com/.

[14] Reas, Casey, and Ben Fry. 2001. "Processing." https://processing.org/.

[15] Rifkin, Jeremy. 2014. The Zero Marginal Cost Society. Palgrave Macmillan.

[16] Idem.

[17] Deamer, Peggy. 2016. "Architects, Really." In Can Architecture Be an Emancipatory Project?: Dialogues On Architecture And The Left. Zero Books.

PROTOTYPES

DR. DAVID GERBER

Dr. David Jason Gerber is an architect, educator, researcher and serial entrepreneur. His work in practice and academia innovates at the intersection of design, engineering, and computer science and brings to design and architecture enhanced exploration, integration, and articulation through technology.

Dr. Gerber is a professor of architecture and engineering with years of experience in the global practice of architecture, urban design, and technology research and development. His research and professional practice continue to be widely published, cited and exhibited internationally.

Dr. Gerber has degrees from UC Berkeley, the AA in London, Harvard University Graduate School of Design, and has held fellowships at MIT's Media Lab and Harvard University.

DESIGN MAVERICKS AND ARCHITECTURAL MAVENS

There was a conference recently hosted by the Harvard University Graduate School of design focused on the architectural competition. The event included some of the faculty luminaries discussing the benefit to our profession and issues of the business model of the competition, the recent Guggenheim competition, and its thousand-plus entries, and some specific stories of firms like that of Snohetta and many other aspects.[1] It seems there was positivism towards the competition model in summary. Not so tangentially I remembered FOA winning the Yokohama Terminal, a seminal project for so many of us. I remember them walking on water and the aura of their win wafting though the AA Bar. In the context of the days spent at the AA, I am also reminded of many other competition has driven design innovations... the Parc de La Villette entrees, of course, Zaha Hadid's Hong Kong Peak and then the story of her Cardiff Opera House. Here there are too many to list. These are all competitions with a doubt providing architecture with its legacy and significance, and therefore in short shrift, a defense of the architectural competition. In a more contemporary setting, I am reminded every year of the eVolo skyscraper ideas competition, perhaps not in the same category of significance but in the same vein and culture of design via the competition. Then there is the PS1 and its many successful projects and its ability to elevate the careers of so many. It is also worth being further reminded that the design endeavor is always within a competitive setting, whether a literal open, invited or super stars only competition; or simply within an office, a team, or the university studio. Here however despite all the fantastic progress the traditional competition model has brought to our profession and discourse, I would like to reflect upon and admittedly espouse the other modes and models of practice.

'Design Mavericks and Design Mavens' sets out to promote, or in the least qualify the importance of other novel models and paradigms for design. It is also recognition and an acquiescing to the cyclicality of those who are at one time the design 'hipsters' inevitably become the squares, the norm, and the standard. In other words in declaring the outsider or of being avant-garde or those coming from behind in your 'Blind-spot,' we also must realize that these 'design mavericks' must strive to stay there or risk becoming the standard. Migayrou's Pompidou curation of the 'Architecture Non-Standard' is an exhibition manuscript I refer to frequently to illustrate the classification of the non-standard in its geometric terms but also as an example for my teams to discern the maverick and maven aspects of the included individual designers.[2] In spite of this waxing and waning of who is our design hipster, of who constitutes the new, the avant-garde, the non-standard, the bleeding edge there are numerous exemplars of design practices and individuals who maintain their preeminence and for being mavericks of design with and without the competition as their primary vehicle for exploration. This cyclicality is Darwinian and the evolution from maverick to cultural meme[3] is a reasonable and essential process within design and consumer cultures.

In part instigated by a direct reflection on the notion of the "Blind-spot" and in part a reaction to the instigation to address non-conformal modes of practice and perhaps specifically the design practice through competition model, this essay highlights alternative design modes and models, and in the parlance of contemporary debate alternative lifestyles. Alternative design lifestyles are prevalent and pervasive as seen through those involved in the design endeavor and design inquiry beyond normative practice. We see this in architectural practices, in specialist consultancies inside these practices and outside, in labs academic and industry, in networks social, anonymous, and rhizomatic, in startups and big corporations alike. On the one hand those reflected upon in the essay are primarily architects or those who have been raised and groomed within Architecture and on the other, they all seem to have a highly developed sense for being mavericks either within the confines of the profession or by stepping outside the norms. In all cases there is something that sets them apart, this includes business models, inane design talent, inventions, and I would argue in most cases a motivation, generically reduced to the notion of being able to control their destiny as designers, that challenges the status quo.

As an important not so aside, the design endeavor is Research. It is requisite of analysis, hypothesis -to certain degrees worthy of debate- and most importantly criticality and synthesis. Design is however unique in that it is equally problem definition and problem-solving. In this context, we would suggest Design Mavericks bring unique creativity and vision for problem definition whereas and not necessarily exclusively Design Mavens bring expertise in solving the design challenge. Fundamentally, the design mavericks' success is a unique combination of both ingenuity, blue-sky creativity and the supporting cast of expert mavens. Those who have avoided being relegated to the norm to becoming standard to losing their hipness, possess some neural 'design' plasticity and in some cases this is seemingly boundless. This plasticity is in large part a fundamental sustaining of curiosity, which directly correlates with the generation of innovation. Here it is not simply new for newness sake but rather new as a result of dissatisfaction with the standard, the status quo, and the norm.

What is architecture without research? What is innovation without the challenging of status quo? Arguably the disassociation of design from research is a misnomer and a misunderstanding of what design is. This aforementioned 'plasticity' is predicated on a desire to ask and answer questions to face challenges and opportunities with often a productive reckless abandon. We wrestle incessantly with the distinction of what constitutes research and what constitutes design; of what a Ph.D. by design is versus a Ph.D. We, as designer researchers, wrestle with and tend to openly reject disciplinary silos and how 'fields' are defined through somewhat arbitrary boundaries, mostly coming from the sciences and its' hermeneutics and historical evolution. Important to note is that the sciences are also experiencing a highly productive blurring of these historical delineations just see the new departments and emphasis on multi-disciplinarily and transformational cluster hires. At the same time, it is critical to maintaining a disciplinary core competency and duty of care, as is suggested by a recent Schumacher prevarication and reminder to us all of Architecture's responsibility to "communicate" and "spatially organize." In large respect, my own mode of design inquiry is continuously a balancing act of work in the hypothesis-driven scientific method- in search of objectivity empiricism, and repeatability, in search of fundamental knowledge and broader impacts- with that of the explorative and open-ended synthetic work that defines and elevates the essentialism of design. The 'sweet spot', an intentional play with the idea of the 'Blind-spot,' occurs when the mix of science and design enable new formal performances. Where performance is equally a discovery of intricacy in design complexity, and nuance in design, and where it is perceived and measured to be performing across the myriad of highly coupled goals; societal, environmental, ecological, and ever more cybernetic, in subjective and objective forms alike.

What is becoming evident is that the convergence of these mindsets, the mad maven scientist, and the maverick.
Creative is finally being valued as highly comingled. In that regard, I would suggest it is by being both a maverick, an out of the box and idiosyncratic creative, a rebel to some extent, in conjunction with being expert, that of a maven, that we see the propulsion of design into the foreground. This foreground is an ever-pressing issue, as we witness the value of architecture and design needing to move out of the self-referential hermeneutic discourse we often find ourselves in. Moving the discourse to both being one of self-reflection and as research as experts in our field inclusive of core competency but equally of being able to speak to and for impacting the quotidian.

We see this foregrounding of design in many forms of practice, in many forms of consultancies, in tech businesses, and in new models of education. There is much to be optimistic about. While the Architectural profession has been passed over and diminished in many ways, it is experiencing resilience and resurgence perhaps a virtue of technological integration but also perhaps because the value of design ability and ingenuity is experiencing its resurgence in direct opposition. Designers are being valued at the upper echelon of corporations finally. At Apple Inc. an impactful first has occurred, a new title has been given to Jony Ives. He has been elevated to that of 'Chief Design Officer,' and likely soon others will follow.[5] We have also seen the rise of the position of Chief Experience Officer or CXO' become another executive role requisite of design education and ability. Equally strong are examples where the likes of Google Inc. have elevated the importance of design and urban systems by formulating Sidewalk labs.[6] I expect we will see Facebook follow suit in some fashion.

The provocation for this discussion is in part based on my trajectory and the many colleagues I have worked with, educated and or competed with over the last 20 years. In other words 'Blindspot', has instigated a reflective pause and brought to bear some categorizing of design Icons and those laying in wait. Within the stints I have had I have come across so many masterful classmates, colleagues, designers, architects, engineers, computer scientists, tinkerers, entrepreneurs, mavericks, and mavens of all kinds. Included in this list are the luminaries Frank Gehry, Moshe Safdie, William J Mitchell, Patrik Schumacher, Greg Lynn, Brett Steele, and Zaha Hadid to name but a few. Then there are the countless others who are more easily categorized as the 'up and coming', as the 'young' and those more clearly in the 'Blind Spot' of the design media especially. Here I would include colleagues and friends such as Casey Reas[7], Jose Sanchez[8], Satoru Sugihara[9] , Alvin Huang[10], Shajay Bhooshan[11], Neri Oxman[12] , and Jenny Sabin[13], all of whom are quintessential examples of working by their standards. Their unique design inquiry and modes of design-research each have lead to innovations and new definitions of practice, some more alternative than others. What has become ever more apparent is the impact and success they have all achieved is in large part a challenging of the status quo, an intense curiosity, a willingness to fail, to not let fear drive their unique design discourses, and a resolute focus on the design-research endeavor. In this list, there are those who have stepped away from traditional modes of practice and there are those who have stepped up the 'normative' mode of practice. What is evident is a rapid proliferation of design ingenuity beyond that of purely the architectural professions

competition model.

f we understand design to require individuality, creativity, and in effect idiosyncrasy then being maverick is essential. If we understand design to be a synthetic métier, one requisite of general knowledge and one requisite of expertise and dexterity, then equally being a maven is essential. The challenge is always to be both, a designer with breadth and depth; moreover, to do so where the accumulation of expertise and technical skill does not become cause for design stagnation and fixation, to be unconstrained by too much technical expertise and yet to be equipped enough to deliver with precision. The Design Mavericks' are those who have a penchant for inventing, making, innovating uniquely within the nexus of the cyber, physical, social. The 'Design Mavens' are those who develop and maintain expertise in the specific fields, methods, tools, and techniques of design. We recently published a book titled Paradigms in Computing, Making, Machines, and Models for Design Agency in Architecture[14] in which we sought and curated a set of designers to put forward the question whether computing is creating a singularity or multiplicity, homogeneity or heterogeneity of paradigms for those involved in any design endeavor. What became clear is there are many modes, methods, and models for working toward the betterment of design processes and design products.

There is an irony to the notion of the alternative design practice' as once upon a time Ms. Zaha Hadid was labeled the paper architect, the design diva, and for sure a maverick with a not so veiled up turned nose of exclusion, and now she is arguably in professional terms one of the worlds leading designers and principle of an architectural practice perhaps ironically now considerably mainstream. Her firm was named the Practice of the year beating out Hopkins and Foster and Partners.[15] Frank Gehry, the architect of the Facebook Headquarters, remains a maverick at the age of 85. He challenged Zuckerberg to allow him to compete for the project on price knowing he had a team of mavens lying in wait. Greg Lynn, another maverick and maven in one; arguably an iconic designer and main theoretical influence of a generation of architects, adept at re theorizing architecture and design as well as applying expertise on the machines. Patrik Schumacher another who has tirelessly put forward theoretical discourses challenging the status quo all the while building a portfolio of research and built work arguably near impossible to contest. Then there are countless others who may not hold an Oscar, or a Prizker per se but are quintessentially design mavericks omitted only for lack of time. As with any discussion of what or who is the hip, the hipsters, the alternative, we must acknowledge a cycle of eating ones young. Kurt Cobain can be heard in elevators and the once "radical" and "paper" architect Zaha Hadid can be argued now as a global brand; walk around almost any school of design and her work along with the others mentioned here will be displayed almost ad nausea. What is at issue is to realize that there is always an underlying set of characteristics that can describe a proliferation of alternative design practices and outlets... it is a sense of being a maverick both from within the system and or being on the outside, as well as a perpetual drive to maintain control and expertise in one's domain and therefore maven status

So in discussing the alternative design modes, the design studio model is our de facto standard. It is the model of design practice that we have been instigated to reflect upon. It is a mode historically built on the competition model and whenever possible direct commission. The example I would like to use is that of Greg Lynn's studio where his design sensibility and persistent pushing of the technical the dynamic, processes, and of materiality in architecture has moved away from the normal limitations of an architect's representational realm and delved directly into the "no no" of means and methods. He is a design maverick to the core, influencing an entire generation of architects but equally pushing his envelope beyond just architecture as is seen in his most recent work "Girl Friend" GF 42, a predominantly carbon fiber composite performance driven trimaran. Another mode and more recently novel model is that of the Research and Development group. They have been a part of corporate budgets for a long while and have now tricked down to the design firms, finally. We can see these units at the large global firms and in those labeled as the avant-garde; Norman Fosters' SMG (Specialist Modeling Group), SOM's Blackbox, Frank Gehry's eponymous Gehry Technologies, and ZHA CODE are just a few worth mentioning on this spectrum. However, before all of these, there was The Skunk Works[16] with its ethos of secrecy, of the clandestine, of national urgency and security, and of a fearless commitment to solving the engineering challenges of supersonic flight and space travel. In some ways Norman Fosters' SMG has built up this allure, arguably because they rarely like to give away competitive advantage, others I believe to be more genuinely skunk work like are the design organizations internal to Google X or Apple Inc. lead by Jony Ives.

Then there are the 'Lone Wolves' where Ross Lovegrove comes to mind or an Ai Wei Wei or an Anish Kapoor. They are all maverick design icons in their rights whether the work is considered design or art. However, for this category, there is a blurring of the lines between individual and the studio, as they all are supported by teams of swarming mavens of experts internally and externally. Another important category is that of the laboratory with its clear origins in the scientific method and heritage though now applied as a label in a much more liberal and arguably more productively multi-faceted fashion. Here there are so many labs worth mentioning those within academic organizations and those extrinsic; XEROX Parc, Bell Labs the Media Lab at MIT, the i-lab at USC, and perhaps even the Media Arts Lab, the skunk works for Apple's advertising agency. Closer to home is a set of educational programs that have exhibited a sense for the disruption and 'mavericism' such as the AA Design Research Laboratory, and the Southern California Institute of Architecture a school established through an anti establishment manifesto by a clear cadre of maverick architects and designers. The idea of the lab as a place for unabashed research and experimentation is equally a maverick endeavor within the normal constraints of both the profession and the normalizing and sometimes numbing constraints of curriculum. The results of many of these programs are astonishing in objective terms. The product of which are graduates, designers, who have gone on to critical acclaim as individuals or as the mavens instrumental to the architects, and companies alike.

The purpose here is not to rebel against one's profession but rather to highlight the productive proliferation of those educated and raised within our professional settings as genuinely maverick influencers of all things designed. Frank Gehry, Zaha Hadid, Thom Mayne, all Pritzker prize-winning architects all with global architectural practices were and arguably still are all mavericks. What is also evident is they have built around them teams of mavens to support their individual synthetic and idiosyncratic design processes. Where Gehry has gone on to build Gehry Technologies, and Zaha and Patrik Schumacher have ZHA CODE while maybe mainstream now, are in effect maverick moves now copied by so many others. The one request in formulating the work was not to relate to the notion of the

'Blindspot' per se but rather to recount an alternative or alternative design "lifestyles" to that of the competition-driven practices. In that regard it is clear from the cast of characters included here that there is a myriad of alternative modes, models, and practice formulations that break with the traditional competition only mode of practice. While this is a trite conclusion, what I would in turn highlight is that there is a reason for continued optimism in the resurgence of design being valued not only in the 'avant-garde' but more and more so in the mainstream.

http://www.gsd.harvard.edu/#/events/the-design-competition-conference.html

[2] Mark Burry, Zeynep Mennan, Frédéric Migayrou, Walter Prigge, Centre national d'art et de culture Georges Pompidou, Architectures non standard (Exposition, exposition présentée au Centre Pompidou, Galerie Sud, 10 déc. 2003-1er mars 2004) 2003 Edition : Paris, France, Centre Pompidou 223 p. ; ill. en noir et en coul. ; 29 cm français ISBN : 2-84426-231-7

[3] Richard Dawkins (1989). The Selfish Gene (Paperback ed.). Oxford University Press. ISBN 9780192860927

[4] Patrik Schumacher: "The Denunciation of Architectural Icons and Stars is Superficial and Ignorant" https://www.facebook.com/patrik.schumacher.10/posts/10205380818112860 (Accessed 6/15/2015

[5] http://techcrunch.com/2015/05/25/apple-names-jony-ive-chief-design-officer/

[6] http://sidewalkinc.com/

[7] http://reas.com/

[8] http://www.plethora-project.com/

[9] http://atlv.org/

[10] http://synthesis-dna.com/

[11] http://block.arch.ethz.ch/brg/people/shajay-bhooshan

[12] http://www.materialecology.com/

[13] http://jennysabin.com/

[14] Gerber D, Ibanez M. (2014) "Paradigms in Computing: Making, Machines, and Models for Design Agency in Architecture," eVolo (408 pages). ISBN: 978-1938740091

[15] http://www.architectsjournal.co.uk/home/events/zaha-bags-aj120-international-practice-of-the-year-award/8684141.article

[16] http://www.lockheedmartin.com/us/aeronautics/skunkworks.html

ATLV

SATORU SUGIHARA

Satoru Sugihara is a principal and founder at the computational design firm ATLV founded in 2012. Before his firm, he worked at Morphosis as a computational designer, at DR_D and Greg Lynn FORM as an architectural designer, and at IMRF in Tokyo as a researcher in media art. He is a faculty at SCI-Arc teaching computational design seminars. He taught computational design at the University of British Columbia, Paris-Malaquais, Woodbury University and Tokyo University of the Arts.

FIG 2.1 Layers of transparent acrylic sheets with organically shaped holes cast shadows on the floor showing the cloudiness of the whole form and materials.

ndspot Initiative

2.1

A(G)NTENSE

A(g)ntense installation is an experiment to take a step forward in research of agent-based computational design integrating swarm agents and structural self-optimizing agents.

A swarm agent algorithm generates self-organized formation through agents' movement with consistent steering to have a certain distance relationship and simultaneously responds to obstacles and external force fields like gravity or attractors. For the installation to be produced with physical materials, this swarm formation algorithm is integrated with self-optimizing agent algorithm to deal with materials' structural behaviors under gravity. In the installation, trajectory lines of swarm agents are translated into high strength fishing wires to be tensile structure and connection lines between adjacent agents form compression structural network on each horizontal layer which is fabricated as a CNC-cut acrylic sheet. The tensile wires penetrate through all the horizontal acrylic sheets hanging them and acrylic sheets keep the distance relationship of the swarm agents' trajectories. However, without taking gravity and structural behaviors into consideration in the agent design, the horizontal sheet materials hung by irregularly distributed wires in various diagonal angles would not stay horizontal but instead would tilt, twist and deform the overall form generated by the agents. To minimize deformation and torsion under gravity, the swarm agents creates tension line agents on the trajectories, compression line agents on the horizontal linkage, and node agents to connect them. These agents simulate structural behaviors under gravity and constantly readjust trajectory lines and connection lines optimizing their structural behaviors to minimize deformation and to keep the horizontal layer perfectly horizontal. Through these self-optimizing agent algorithms, the self-organized formation generated through the agents' interaction registers the structural insight. The networked formation of tensile lines and compression lines generated from this algorithm should show a stable structural behavior in real physical space with gravity as simulated and optimized.

The physical installation is built to prove the effectiveness of the agent-based structural self-optimization algorithm. The agent's formation is digitally and systematically translated into 31 layers of outline drawings for laser cutting CNC-fabrication of acrylic sheets. The self-optimized 153 trajectory lines of swarm agents are also translated into another set of drawings for fabrication of fishing wires with exact spacing for joints with the horizontal acrylic sheets. The acrylic sheets are cut with a set of big holes as part of networking formation and another set of small holes for intersectional joints with fishing wires. All joint holes are labeled with wire ID number for assembly process. The 153 wires are hung from the ceiling penetrating 31 layers of acrylic sheets. These wires penetrating 31 layers are divided into four sections of the ceiling to the 1st layer / from 1st – 11th / from 11th to 21st / from 21st to 31st to make the assembly process comfortable and flexible. As result total, 124 segments of wires are fabricated with joints for the acrylic sheets. The joint of fishing wires and acrylic sheets are designed to be made out of two interlocking metal rings and a small slot on an acrylic sheet for quick and efficient assembly. One of two metal rings is tied to the fishing wire and another one is kept loose with the wire inside the ring. This makes these two rings quickly pass through the slot on the sheet by pushing them but not easily come back up by pulling because two rings naturally interlock each other at the back side of the slot. For 153 wires to intersect with 31 sheets, it needs 153 x 31 = 4743 joints. It also needs joints for the ceiling and ones between 4 sections and the total number of joints are 5508. 124 segments of wires with 5508 joints tied at all unique locations

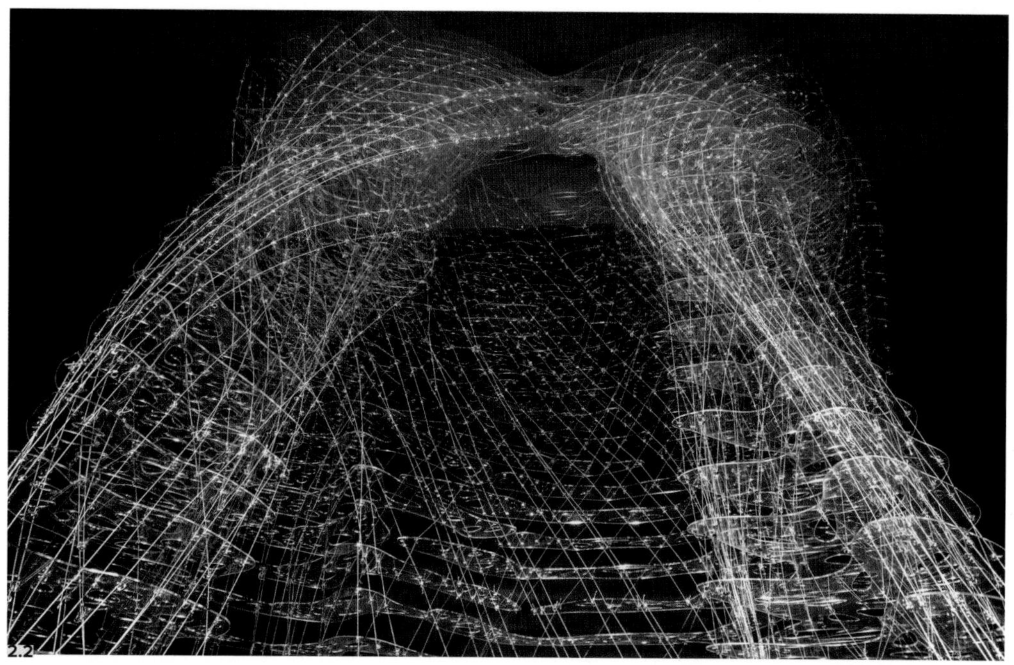
2.2

are fabricated by hand with assistance of 22 contributors.

Laser-cut acrylic sheets are assembled by putting through the wires hung from the ceiling and also through the joint rings. The sheets were installed from top to bottom. As the lower sheets are installed on the wires, gravity naturally forms the shape and formation the agents generated in the algorithm and simulation and all sheets were installed all horizontally and stably. This successful assembly of the installation as designed by agents proved the effectiveness of the agent-based self-optimizing algorithm.

Conventionally in wire-suspended physical structure for horizontal layers, horizontal layers express its form and wires function purely structurally and stay in the background. In A(g)ntense installation, the wires primarily express the trajectory of swarm movement and the horizontal layers function as structure to hold the wires on each level. Also, to function as structure, horizontal layers need to have specific shapes which are directly generated from the formation of the swarm on each level and when those shapes are stacked together, the organic form surrounding the swarm trajectory emerges. This secondarily generated form by horizontal layers continually expresses itself while swarm trajectory by the tensile wires does simultaneously. Because of the form generation process, they are perfectly aligned together, but at the same time, each of them expresses its characteristics refusing to converge into one. This dual expression blurs human perception to claim the new relationship of tensile materials and compression materials in wire-suspended layer structure. This new relationship is made possible by computational design process with self-optimization agent algorithms.

Credits
Photography: Taiyo Watanabe

Fabrication Assistance:
Matheos Asfaw, Prajakt Karmarkar, Jun Ding, Thomas Legleu, Hao Wu, Daniel Berdichevsky, Shuangzhi Shen, Yulun Wu, Ou Liu, Andrew Choi, Salvador Cortez, Avra Tomara, Alex Chang, Kevin Nguyen, Mohammed Aljehani, Viola Ago, Federico, Pessani, Sahng O Lee, Nanao Shimizu, Robbie Mehring, Setareh Ordoobal, Guoyu Hu.

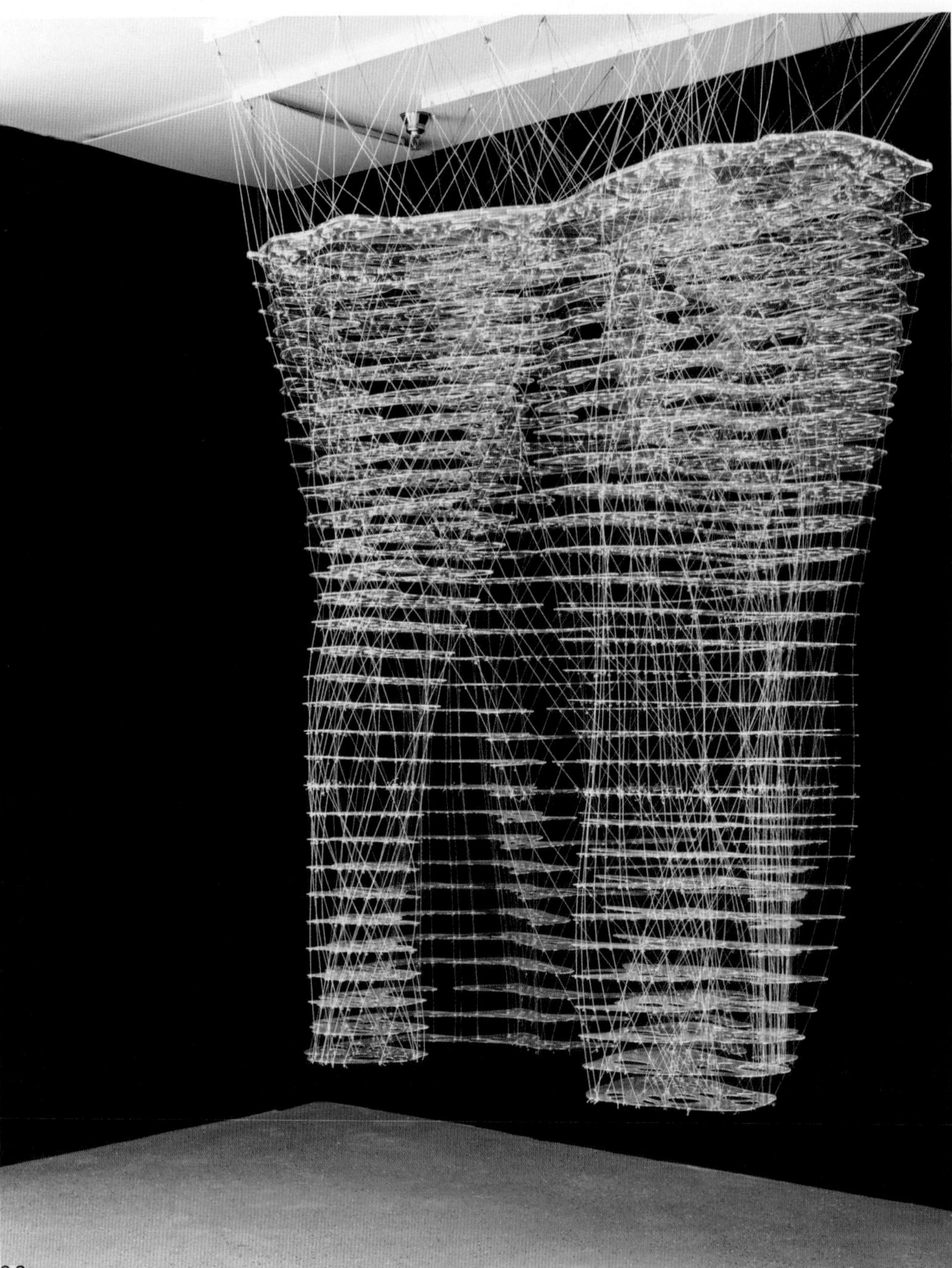

2.3

Fig. 2.2 The groups of force fields at the two poles push swarm into the two clusters forming column forms and one cluster forming back woven surface form, to make the central void space as result of the self-organization.

Fig. 2.3 The tensile wires are not only structural but also expressive showing the dynamic flow of swarm agents. On the other hand, the horizontal sections automatically generated from the swarm formation express the organic form surrounding the swarm trajectory. They show the new relationship between horizontal layer materials and tensile wire structure being both independently expressive and structural.

2.4

Fig. 2.4 The trajectories of swarm movement influenced by the virtual force fields created the void space in the middle in which one person can fit.

Fig. 2.5 The tensile wires express the dynamic movement of swarms, gathering to form clusters, keeping distance between each other and influenced by swirling force fields simultaneously. There are two groups of swarm which were implemented by white and black fishing wire. These two groups of swarm move independently and swirl in the opposite direction.

In the design process, the swarm agent simulation was executed from the top to the bottom. On the very top, the swarm agents are randomly and equally distributed and towards the bottom they self-organize and make clusters.

2.5

GILLES RETSIN

Gilles Retsin is the founder of Gilles Retsin Architecture, a young awardwinning London based architecture and design practice investigating new architectural models which engage with the potential of increased computational power and fabrication to generate buildings and objects with a previously unseen structure, detail and materiality. The studio is interested in the impact of computation and new fabrication methods on the core principles of architecture – the bones rather than the skin. The practice has developed numerous provocative proposals for international competitions, qualifying most recently as one of the finalists for the international competition for the New National Gallery in Budapest. His work has been acquired by the Centre Pompidou in Paris, and has been exhibited internationally in museums such as the Museum of Art and Design in New York.

Gilles graduated from the Architectural Association in London. Before founding his practice, he worked in Switzerland as a project architect with Christian Kerez, and in London with Kokkugia. He also co founded SoftKill Design, a collective design studio investigating generative design methodologies for additive manufacturing and 3Dprinting, credited with the first design for a 3D printed house. Alongside his practice, Gilles directs a research cluster at UCL/ the Bartlett School of Architecture investigating robotic manufacturing and largescale 3D printing.

3.1

BLOKHUT

Blokhut: Dutch for Log Cabin. A hut built of whole or split logs.[1]

What does it mean for buildings or material organizations to be discrete and digital? Can material be organized in the same way as data? Analog fabrication is based on continuously aggregating material with an infinite connection scheme. Whereas digital or discrete fabrication is based on assembling parts, which the geometry provides metrics and constraints, limiting the connection scheme to a precise digit: yes or no.[2] *3D printing, just as CNC milling, is fundamentally a continuous fabrication process, which may leave us with an interesting form at the end, but fundamentally produces objects which are completely analog. A 3D printed vase, which may have been generated with a complex algorithm, is still going to be analog once printed. The organization of material is in all cases the same: it is a continuous extrusion of material, sintered or stuck together with a binder, and it has no relation to the underlying computational process. As a continuous method, 3D Printing fundamentally suffers from scalability, structural problems such as cantilevers, and more importantly, it has a big problem with multi-materiality.*[3] *For example, a process which can print at the same time glass and concrete, is hard to imagine, as both materials require different printing techniques. This means that even if a building would be printed out of concrete, one would still have to rely on ideas of assemblage to incorporate insulation, transparency, finishes, etc. On the other hand, it is easy to imagine a prefabricated brick consisting of multiple layers of materials, such as a structural layer, a layer of insulation, waterproofing, finishing and so on.*

An assembly based process has the potential to differentiate the materiality of parts and particles, introducing transparency, electrical conductivity, channels for air or water flow, all on different recursive scales. With discrete fabrication, the part computed digitally is also the part assembled physically. The organization of physical parts is the same as the organization of the digital data.

The "Blokhut" (2014) was developed as a case study of aligning discrete computation and discrete fabrication. Initially a study for a villa in a Belgian suburb, the design became an independent research project prototypical for a new approach towards computational design. The prototype started out with a given: due to a limited budget, a large part of the structure would have to be standardized and made out of cheap elements. The large model of 2x1.5x0.3m, weights over 150 kg and is built using 4000+ pre-cast plaster components, intersecting and joining around a limited number of customized, 3D printed zones. The plaster component is designed as an arrow-shaped brick, with a male and female connection. The arrow-like connection can interlock two bricks together in a fixed position. This discrete arrow-shaped building element can be understood as digital material. The design possibility or how elements can combine and aggregate is defined by the geometry of the element itself - which leads to a "tool-less" assembly. (Cheung 2012) The Blokhut prototype establishes a differentiated and adaptive architectural system which consists of 90% of serially repeated, discrete, prefabricated concrete elements, and for 10% of unique, customized 3D-printed pieces. The argument shifts from a system where everything is mass customized, with a labor-intensive assembly process, to a limited number of super intensive, rule-changing customized zones or glitches and a large number of serially repeated, cheap

3.2

material. The finished state of the model is undetermined. It can be extended or contracted at any time. The final geometry is messy, redundant and un-simplified. The Blokhut prototype can be constructed without the need for micro-managing thousands of unique, numbered pieces. Instead, the 3D printed components and bricks set out the instructions for assembly. The assembly is "plan-less" and "tool-less," as the geometry of the pieces defines the aggregation. The Blokhut prototype proves that serial repetition of straightforward, cheap, prefabricated digital materials is a feasible and accessible method to achieve complete and adaptable spaces. After the initial prototype for the Blokhut, several more test cases were developed. In a speculative proposal for a building at the Karlsplatz in Vienna, the bricks construct a series of horizontal strata which develop into large, column-like elements. Another abstract atrium-like model was developed which shows how an entirely different spatial structure can be achieved with the same method.

[1] Oxford Dictionaries [online][accessed 22.10.2015] Available from: http://www.oxforddictionaries.com/definition/english/log-cabin

[2] Kenneth Cheung, Neil Gerschenfeld T*he geometry of the parts being assembled provides the dimensional constraints required to precisely achieve complex forms. (Cheung)*

[3] The Objet printer gradually differentiates stiffness and color within one material.

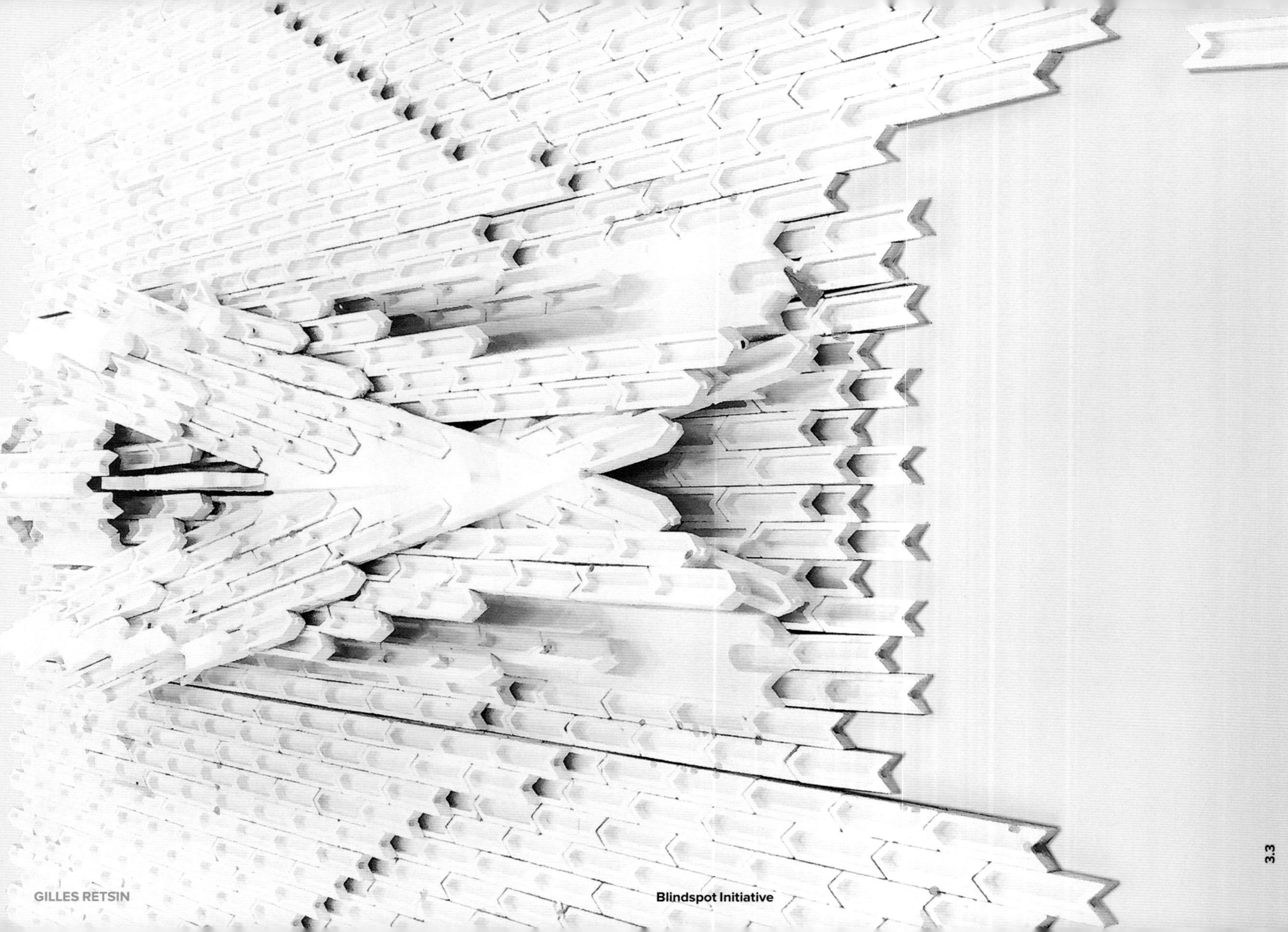

3.3

3.4

3.5

Fig. 3.2 – 3.3 Bottom half of the Blokhut prototype assembly. The prototype consists of 4000+ precast plaster tiles, assembled around a limited number of customised, 3D printed intersections.

Fig. 3.4 Design Study for an atrium using the Blokhut construction method. The design explores a more organic language compared to the Blokhut prototype.

Fig. 3.5 "KarlsPlatz" Study for a building at the Karlsplatz in Vienna. This study explores the versatility of the Blokhut system to generate different kinds of spaces and typologies using the same design method. This version establishes articulated columns and beams which transition into thick, volumetric floor slabs.

Blindspot Ini
3.6

indspot

MICHAEL KONTOPOULOS

Michael Kontopoulos is an artist, designer, and storyteller working at the intersection of interactive media and conceptual art. His ongoing studio work draws heavily on themes and strategies in Science Fiction literature and typically explores the creation of fictitious characters, systems or machines. By exploring sculptural prototypes through short films and photographs, his work questions what conditions of social want or need could drive people to invent objects that critique or subvert the status quo rather than affirm it.

Michael has exhibited solo and collaborative projects in galleries, festivals and conferences in the U.S., Asia, and Europe, including the Santa Monica GLOW Festival, the Sundance Film Festival, the TED conference, LACE Gallery in Los Angeles, CA. He was the winner of a 2010 Rhizome Commission for Emerging Artists, sponsored by the New Museum of New York. Currently, he teaches programming, electronics and sculpture courses at Art Center College of Design, UCLA, California State University, Long Beach and the University of Southern California. He holds a BFA in Fine Art from Carnegie Mellon University and an MFA in Design and Media Arts from UCLA.

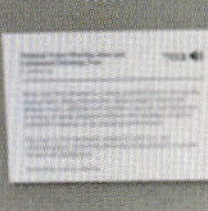

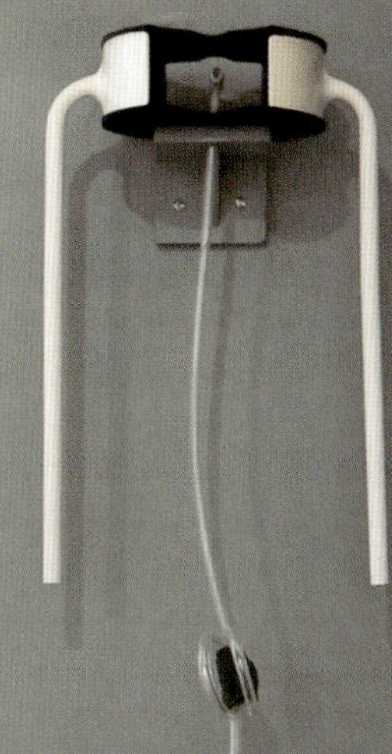

4.1

WATER RITES

Robert Heinlein's celebrated 1961 novel, Stranger in a Strange Land, tells the story of a human baby that is marooned on Mars and raised by native Martians. Upon his return to Earth, he must acclimatize to human culture and customs, including the casual relationship that humans have to water. On his native Mars, an arid planet, the sharing of water with another person is a ceremonial gesture which, when completed, cements the two individuals together with the new and sacred title of "water brother." Science Fiction provides many such examples of encounters between disparate cultures, usually exacerbated by differences in resource management or law. Few of them address, with such perspicacity, the extent to which the extreme scarcity of water – a resource most of us take for granted – can produce and encode such morally-ordered social interactions. Another example from literature is given in Frank Herbert's Dune (1965), where certain curious social gestures develop on the parched fictional planet of Arackis to show respect, such as spitting at the feet of another person in place of hand-shaking (as an offering of your inner water to them).

Speculative fiction holds a mirror to our own culture. It asks us to question our relationship to water, in these cases. In this tradition, Kontopoulos has created Water Rites, a two-channel video and series of artifacts exhibited in two parts: Ritual (2011) and Shrine (2014). Ritual tells the story of two characters who engage in a water-sharing ceremony. Shrine describes a potential process by which drying river beds could be commemorated. Both pieces introduce artifacts from an alternative Los Angeles invented by the artist. Through a combination of diegetic prototypes, photographs, and video, Water Rites explores a slice of uncanny, fictitious culture from a world where our relationship to water is far less cavalier.

Ritual addresses a social, interpersonal response to the diminishing quantity of the resource. Following the logic of Heinlein or Herbert, when something is scarce it becomes culturally precious. Making, moving and most notably, sharing it, carries with it a heightened social significance. The piece is comprised of four devices that are partially electronic (two mobile water-purifying devices, one "altar" and one tool for communal drinking), and a two-channel video installation. Each channel follows one of two individuals–presumably romantic partners–as they prepare a water source for a specific ceremony. The ceremony combines many of the typical stages found in religious and secular rituals.

The decision to combine water sources and drink together is a symbolic act that codifies their relationship and gives it meaning. It is left intentionally ambiguous whether or not this is a ceremony that has been practiced by many people over many years, or just something these two people invented together that has special meaning only to them.

Shrine, is a more direct response to the official 2014 announcement of draught in Los Angeles. These Shrines are based on the design and use of Greek roadside shrines or Kandylakia (Καντηλάκια). Often resembling small houses on precarious metal legs (containing icons, candles, etc.), these Shrines are built or purchased and typically situated at roadside locations adjacent to traffic accidents. Whether the accident was fatal or survived a shrine marks the location and serves as a ritualistic locus for reflecting on the boundary between life and death.

These moisture shrines are designed to adorn dry sites, failed rivers and locations of human-made interventions in the struggling natural world. There are electronics inside

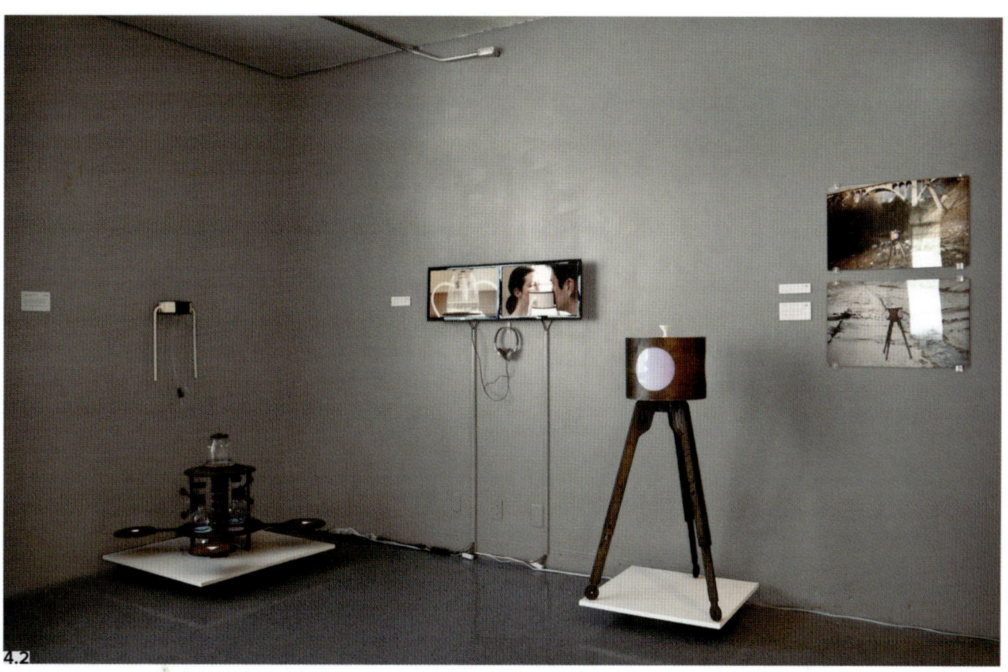
4.2

that detect the moisture level in the shrine and respond with colored lighting. Devotees of the speculative water-based spirituality found in Water Rites might construct or seek out Moisture Shrines to keep them wet. Forfeiting water to the top of the shrine will bring the lighting back to white, from red.

Ultimately, one might ponder: Is this implying a dystopian vision of Los Angeles, considering our current trajectory of poor water management? Could this be ushering us into an alternative present? Perhaps a more appropriate question to ask is: Why would it be surprising if such a practice existed today?

Credits:
Audio: Yiannis Chrisofides
Photography: Christopher O'Leary
Fabrication Assistance: Machine Histories
Actors: Johanna Reed and Mattia Casalegno

4.3

Fig. 4.2 - 4.3 Shrine, from the series Water Rites, is a response to the Los Angeles draught of 2014. These Shrines are based on the design and use of Greek roadside shrines or Kandylakia (Καντηλάκια).

Often resembling small houses on precarious metal legs (containing icons, candles, etc.), these Shrines are built or purchased and typically placed at roadside locations adjacent to traffic accidents. Whether the accident was fatal or survived a shrine marks the location and serves as a ritualistic locus for reflecting on the boundary between life and death.

4.4

Fig. 4.4-4.5 These moisture shrines are designed to adorn dry sites, failed rivers and locations of human-made interventions in the struggling natural world. There are electronics inside that detect the moisture level in the shrine and respond with colored lighting. Devotees of the speculative water-based spirituality found in Water Rites might construct or seek out Moisture Shrines to keep them wet. Forfeiting water to the top of the shrine will bring the lighting back to white, from red.

COMPLICIT MATTER

LUIS QUINONES

Luis Quinones is a computational designer living in Los Angeles. His interests lie in blurring the lines between reality, artificiality and the "Hyper Real." He spent two years as Design Director @ compMatter-TA, a bending discipline group with interests that spanned architecture, computation, design, and media. Formerly a Lead Designer at Emergent Architecture in Los Angeles, Luis specialized in advanced digital and algorithmic design, he was a designer for two winning competitions during his time there. In 2010 Luis founded [n]igma + complicitMatter as a testing ground for design & research across all disciplines, from the macro to the nano.

Luis' research work has been exhibited globally as well as in Popular Science and Future Magazine. He has taught technical, computational and design workshops at Tongji University, Sci-Arc, USC, Texas Tech University, D.O.T.S, and Apo Mechanes in Athens, Greece. Most recently Luis lectured at USC & Tongji University in Shanghai titled 'Total Recall' as part of the Future of DigitalDesign Symposium. His current research focuses on multidisciplinary research and algorithmic processes as design methodologies.

5.1

PARAPRAXIS

PARAPRAXIS is a conceptual geometry study exploring the relationships between perception + mathematically driven computational geometry + human interference. It sets to destroy and mutate a rigid computationally driven geometric system to create a series of Rorschach studies. What starts out as a series of triple periodic minimal surfaces transitions and morphs into the unknown.

Each RSR base sequence is derived from a unique rule set of region construction with enough randomness built in to assure the inability to explicitly replicate.

The glass was chosen as a way to represent the 3Dimensionality of the pieces.

30 Layered RSR Piece is made up of 30 pieces of glass each containing a specific "layer" of the sequence. While the spacing between each glass piece is consistent, each layer does not contain the same amount of information. The 3Dimensional geometric model was cut into slices, 65 of them to be exact. While there were only 30 pieces of glass, each layer did not contain an exact amount of slices. Depending on which areas required more transparency vs. color density or opacity, layers were combined to create the desired effect. The "moment" as we described it was that specific moment in time where this piece was captured as it was exploding from the inside out on a computer simulation. The idea was to capture this almost like it was frozen in a glass cube, highlighting all of its volumetric qualities and color gradients and indexing that moment in time.

Thank you to Makenzie Murphy, J6 Collaborative & NRT Graphics.

Fig. 5.2-5.9 RSR.001 and RSR.002 mark the first 2 in a sequence of 4 RSR series. These are the first mutated sets, certain characteristic and elements from the initial base aggregations were used as drivers for the deformations and transformations. This sequence begins to blur the distinction between the "pure" geometries and begins to explore a territory of perception caused by human interference.

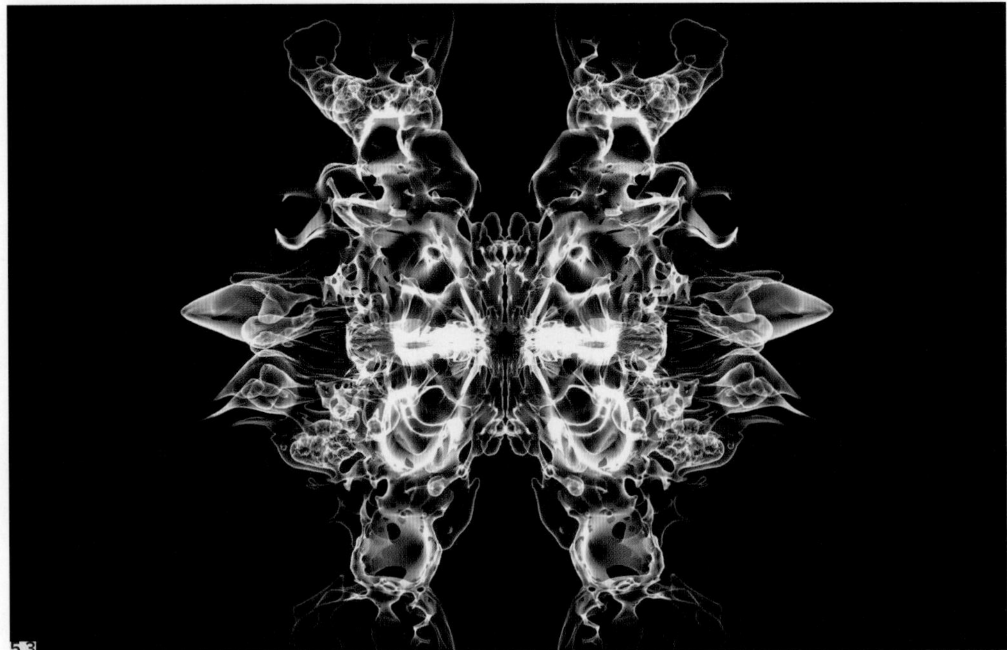

5.3

5.4

Fig. 5.3 – 5.6 Sets of both mutated and normalized triple periodic minimal surfaces aggregated into a cluster. Mutations occurred at all levels with new clusters of aggregations consisting of varying densities. Once the new base clusters were generated, a sequence of 4 was chosen for mutations. These initial geometry studies remained "pure" and unaltered throughout the entire process..

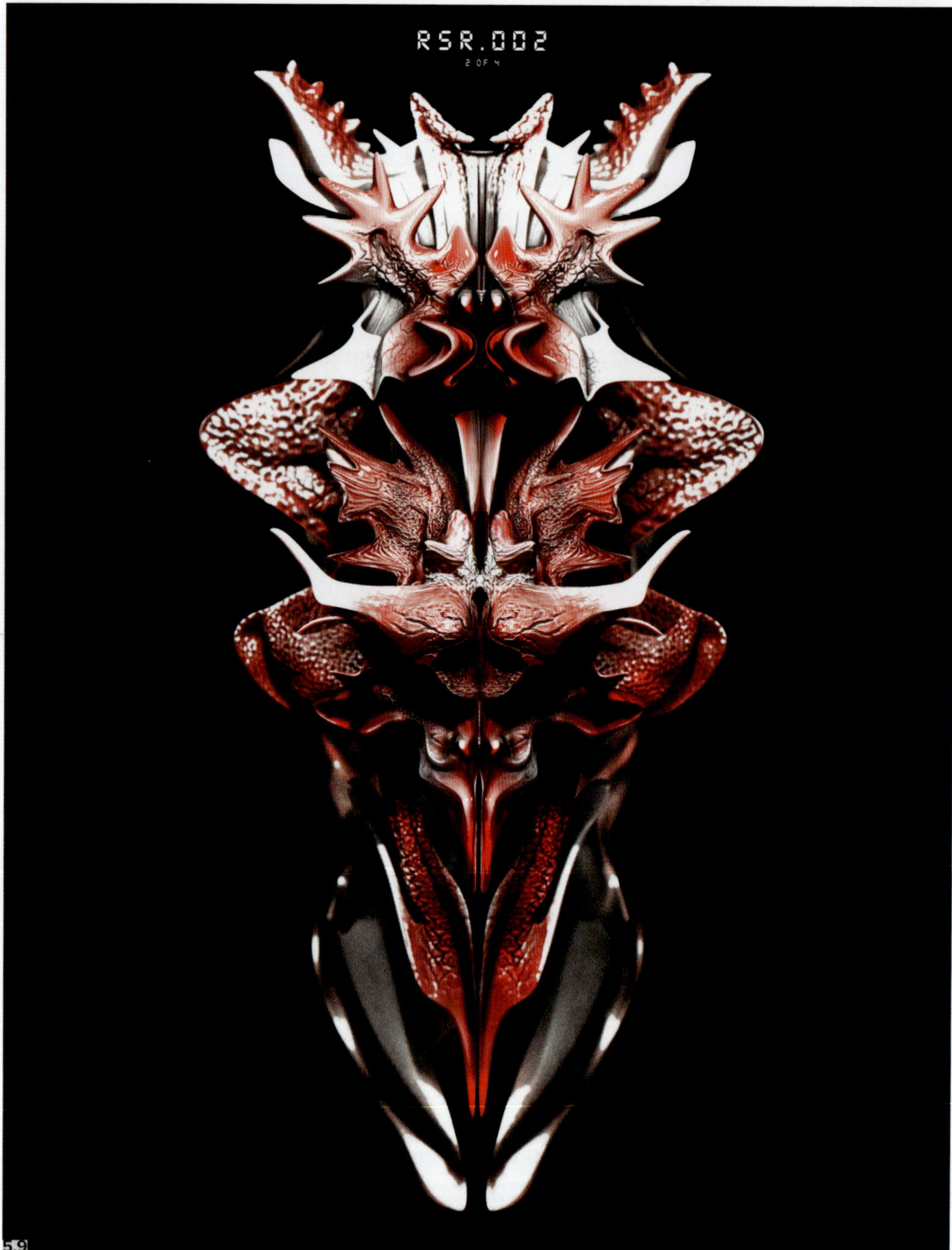

5.9

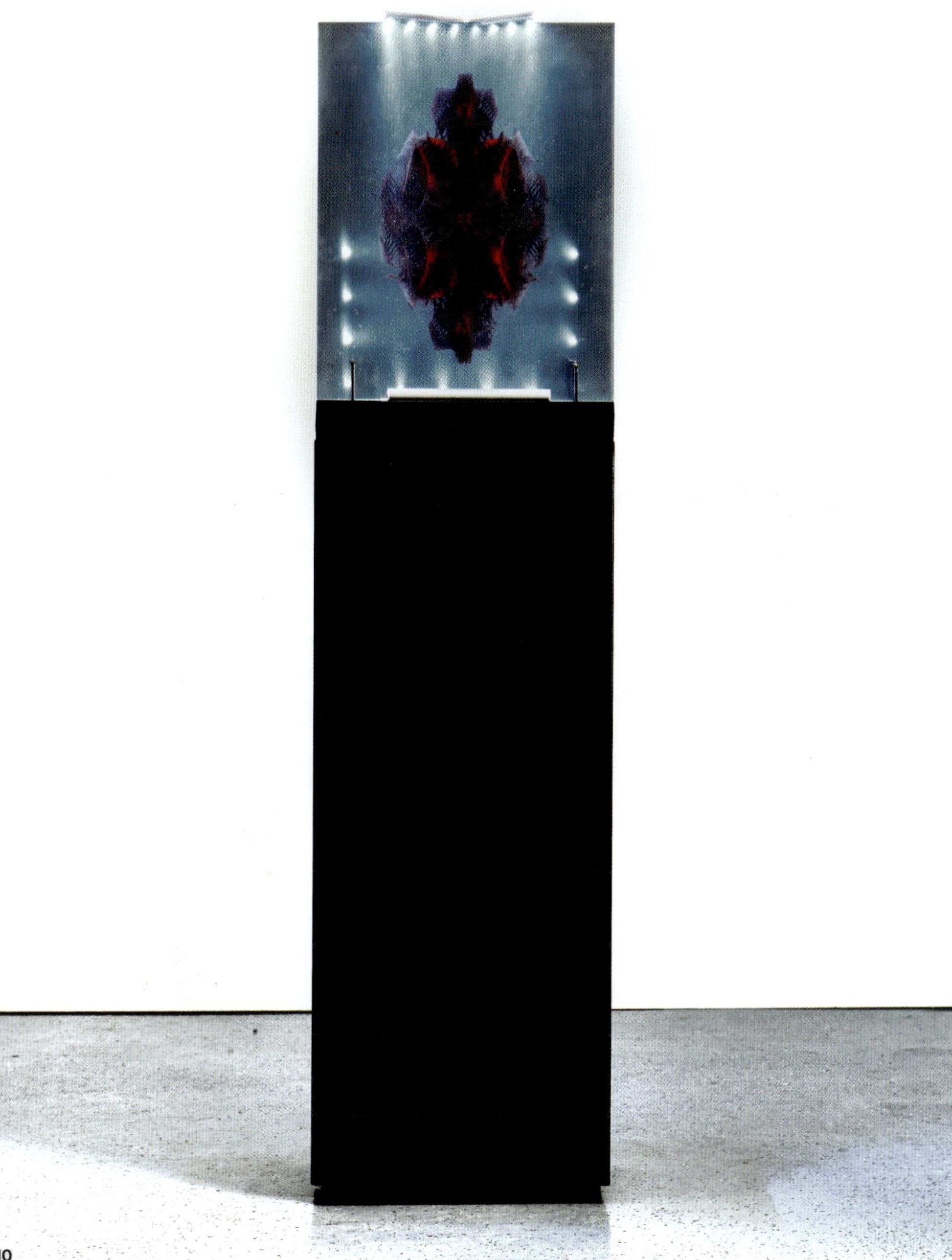

5.10

Fig. 5.10 30 Layered RSR Piece is made up of 30 pieces of glass each containing a specific "layer" of the sequence. While the spacing between each glass piece is consistent, each layer does not contain the same amount of information. The 3Dimensional geometric model was cut into slices, 65 of them to be exact. While there were only 30 pieces of glass, each layer did not contain an exact amount of slices. Depending on which areas required more transparency vs. color density or opacity, layers were combined to create the desired effect.

The "moment" as we described it was that specific moment in time where this piece was captured as it was exploding from the inside out on a computer simulation. The idea was to capture this almost like it was frozen in a glass cube, highlighting all of its volumetric qualities and color gradients and indexing that moment in time.

NICHOLAS HANNA

Nicholas Hanna is an artist and designer who uses his background knowledge as an architect, his identity as a tinkerer and his experience as an artist to create two and three-dimensional artworks that are image, sculpture, installation, and performance all at once. Hanna develops concepts through a methodical process to create works that elicit curiosity and wonder. He seeks beauty and wonders through his work, to explore basic human motivations.

He has exhibited in Los Angeles, Beijing, Shanghai and Hong Kong, most recently as part of an exhibition entitled "Urban Aesthetics" at the Museum of Contemporary Art in Shanghai. He was recognized in 2013 as an emerging artist with an award from the Vilcek Foundation. He holds a Master of Architecture from Yale University, and a Master of Fine Arts from the University of California, Los Angeles (UCLA).

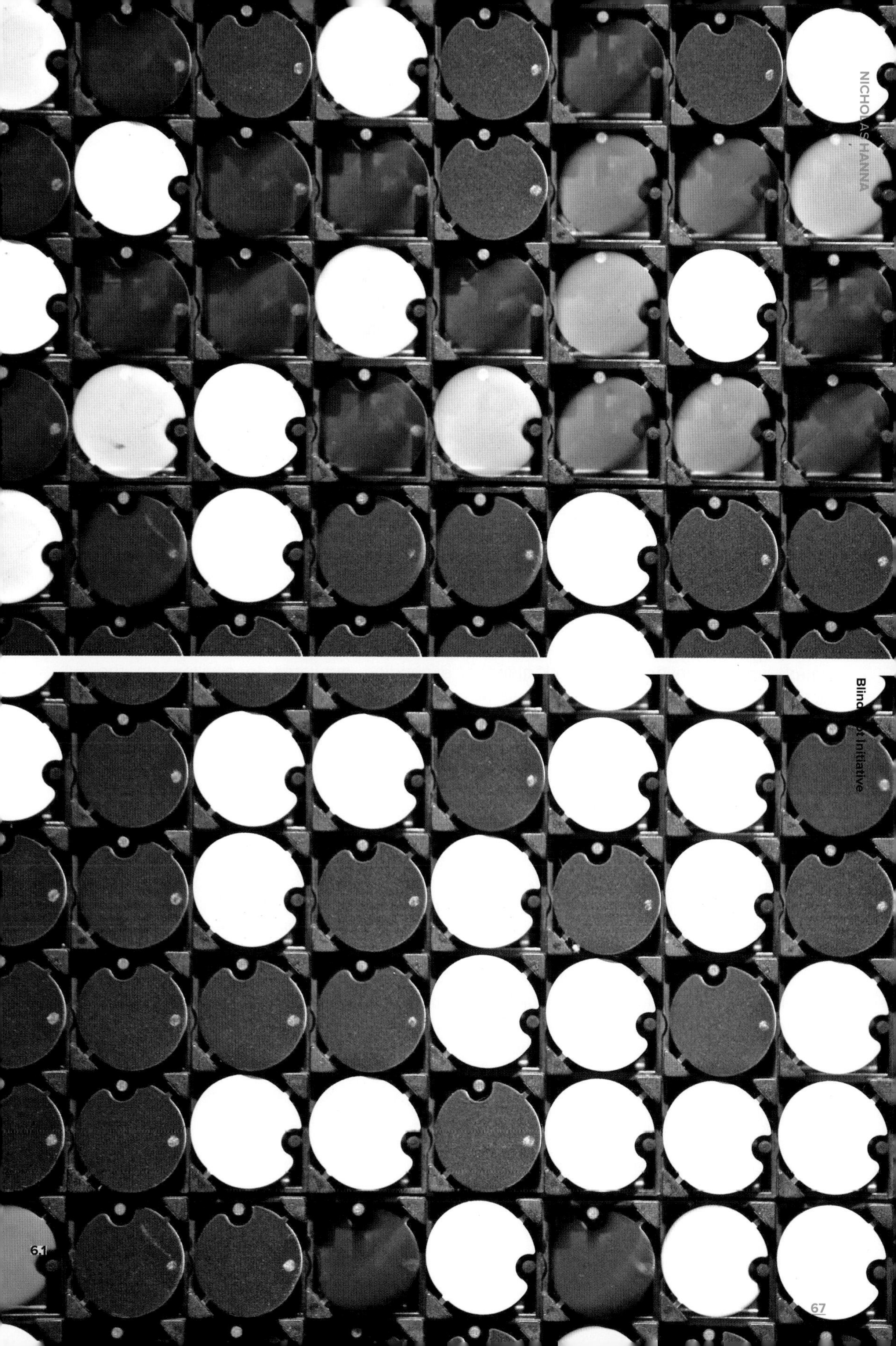

6.1

TWELVE CLOCKS

For ancient humans, time was something that flowed smoothly, marked only by the slow arc of the sun as it moved across the sky from sunrise to sunset. People had only an approximate idea of what time of day it was, what time of year it was, and even how old they were. The invention of the mechanical clock in the 15th century marked a fundamental shift in our relationship with time. Time became a regularized and metered quantity.

Today we live by the clock. We fret over the passing of hours, minutes and even seconds. It is a standard cliché that the pace of life has accelerated. That acceleration is aided by the proliferation of timekeeping instruments: on our walls, in our pockets, and on our computers.

"Twelve Clocks" plays with the convention of the analog clock face. A clock face is a smart, graphical invention: a quick glance at the hands of a clock gives you a sense of where you are in the day. A more detailed examination allows you to fix your time down to the second.

The clocks of "Twelve Clocks" adapt the archetype of the wall clock to represent different scales of time. The first clocks in the series represent time scales faster than a conventional 12-hour clock. The fastest spins once every millisecond (a thousandth of a second). This interval of time lies just below the threshold of our human ability to perceive it. For comparison, the blink of an eye takes about 100 milliseconds. The following clocks in the series mark rhythms that we are more familiar with: one second, one minute, one hour and one day.

This project aims to offer instruments for thinking about and feeling the passage of time. In our accelerated world, it is difficult to think beyond the time of a single day. We may also recognize the rhythm of week and weekend, but do we know what a month feels like?

A year? A decade? The remaining clocks in the series represent time scales that are longer than we are accustomed to in clocks: one week, one month, one year and one decade.

The final clocks represent time scales that are more philosophical. One clock counts down eighty-two years. This symbolizes my life expectancy of eighty-two years as calculated by the United States Social Security Administration.

Another clock marks the years of a millennium, from the year 2000 to 3000. The final clock marks the lifespan of our home: the planet earth. The earth was formed roughly 4.5 billion years ago, and scientists project it will be another 8 billion years until the sun turns into a red giant, expanding outwards to swallow up the earth, boiling off our oceans, and leaving it an uninhabitable rock.

The clocks in this collection are intended to broaden our perception of time so that we can apprehend how we move through measures of time other than the twenty-four hours that are already so well indexed. These new clocks offer a way to experience other measures of time with the same convenience that we can meter the hours of a day. When you look at a conventional, 12-hour clock, you know instantly how long you have been awake, when lunch will be, and how many hours are left until you can go home from work. What does that kind of knowledge do to you at the scale of a week, year, decade or lifetime?

12 clocks – Nicholas Hanna

one microsecond — one second — one minute — one hour

one day — one week — one month — one year

one decade — one lifetime (~82 years) — one millenium — one planet (earth: ~12 billion years)

RANDOM #1

Random #1 is based on an obsolete display technology called a "flip-dot" display panel. The panel is composed of ultra-light disks that are black on one side and white on the other. An electromagnetic coil behind each disk flips the disk around when a current is applied. Before the invention of LED lighting, flip-dot displays were widely used for information display in public places, particularly train stations and airports.

I programmed a microcontroller to interface with the panel. The microcontroller generates a continuous stream of randomness which it sends to the panel. The panel displays this information as a rapidly fluctuating field of black and white dots.

I am intrigued by the humor of using a technology intended for communication to display nonsense. Random #1 tickles the pattern finding facilities of the human mind. The patterns displayed on the panel are in fact anti-patterns: pure randomness. The mind wants to find order and sense in what it is seeing. The experience of looking at Random #1 is like the feeling of being just on the edge of resolving something or figuring something out. It is a visual tease that incites persistent looking.

6.3

6.4

Fig. 6.3 The millisecond clock rotates once every thousand of a second. The motion of its hand is a blur because it spins at 60,000 revolutions per minute.

Fig. 6.4 The earth clock shows the amount of time that has elapsed since scientists calculate the earth was formed, in context of the amount of time remaining until the sun becomes a red giant, expanding outwards to swallow up the earth, boiling off our oceans, and leaving it an uninhabitable rock.

6.5

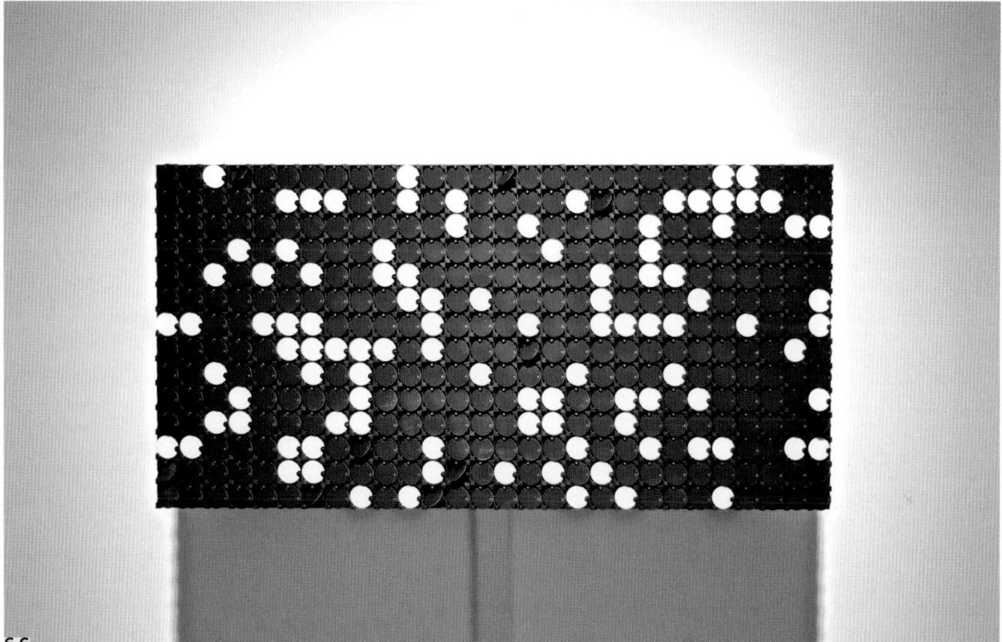

6.6

Fig. 6.5 - 6.6 “Random #1” is made from a flip-dot sign panel unit. A micro-controller running custom software generates randomness and displays it on the panel. While the sequence of black and white disks is purely random, the human mind can't help but discern fragments of pattern in it.

Fig. 6.7 "12 Clocks" from bottom left to top right: microsecond clock, second clock, minute clock, hour clock, day clock, week clock, month clock, year clock, decade clock, lifetime clock, millennium clock, earth clock

2000
2011
2012
2013
2014
2015
2016
2019
1982
2000
2100
2200
2300
2400
2500

SOMEWHERE SOMETHING

BIAYNA BOGOSIAN
JASON KING
ROBBIE MEHRING
SACHA BAUMANN

PLETHORA PROJECT

JOSE SANCHEZ

Somewhere Something is a design firm working at the intersection of art, architecture, computation, fabrication, and education. Integrating emerging technologies as well as traditional design services, they are creating a new model for today's architectural practice. Additionally, they provide computational design consultation and teach the necessary technological skills to design firms.

Jose Sanchez is an Architect / Programmer / Game Designer based in Los Angeles, California. He is a partner at Bloom Games, start-up built upon the BLOOM project, winner of the WONDER SERIES hosted by the City of London for the London 2012 Olympics. He is the director of the Plethora Project (www.plethora-project.com), a research and learning project investing in the future of online open-source knowledge.

Today, he is an Assistant Professor at USC School of Architecture in Los Angeles. His research 'Gamescapes,' explores generative interfaces in the form of video games, speculating in modes of intelligence augmentation, combinatorics, and open systems as a design medium.

7.1

DOT/O

DOT/O is an interactive installation that works as a social experiment/game exploring the capacity and interest of a crowd to 'complete' a suggested structure. The project is inspired by the 'connect the dots' game, where dots with numbers allow a player to discover a hidden drawing by following a sequence. For the installation, the design team developed a steel structure that would act as a host for a crowdsourced threading experience. Users are invited to pick one of the spools of thread stacked on the wall and connect the dots discovering the 3D surfaces that exist between the different frames.

The project was intended to slowly build up density, and use color to map the progress of time and interaction over the structure. Simple rules like maximum distances were suggested but not enforced, allowing players to follow them or ignore them, making the result a combination of order and disorder. The stochastic nature of the installation challenges the idea of formal pre-conceived output, embracing the uncertainty from the social interaction. Slowly, though, the piece would accumulate enough threads where independent intentions would become less visible as a denser and denser fabric would become the dominant collective creation.

While the patterns developed by a single individual with a particular color were very prominent at the beginning of the installation, those motives would slowly become part of a broader trend, one of the probabilistic properties. Most individuals would copy some of the most successful moments attempting to make the piece more coherent and follow a similar language. We could detect a percentage of users that would attempt to leave a unique mark on the piece, one that they could identify with and tell others to see their contribution. This small percentage of individuals was consistent, and one could identify a different behavior at the moment of the gameplay.

The final result is an experimental piece that embraces the messiness of the initial experiment, speculating in the formats and mechanics of crowdsourcing for design. In this regard, we could identify that the piece presents a model of cooperative crowdsourcing, not competitive; while many crowd-sourced projects seek to optimize a design solution by finding a particular individual that can provide the best answer, DOT/O invites all players to be part of the same experience and share the same output. This is a fundamentally different approach and has been dramatically influenced by the work from Aaron Koblin. Koblin, rejects competitive crowdsourcing and generate software platforms that allow many 'workers' (usually through Amazon's mechanical Turk) to construct one new and unique output. In his work as well we can see the emergence of a new kind of esthetic, one that embraces a probabilistic glitch, an unexpected component impossible to forecast as its generated in the contingency of the crowdsourced design process.

Understanding the piece as a social experiment, we should point out to the features that were successful in the sense of the experience intended but also those elements that could have changed allowing for better social engagement. The main misconception of the project has to do with the ability for 'reversibility.' If you look at games like LEGO, one of the key features is to be able to generate trial and error, allowing the user to learn and re-iterate and improve its design. This was not possible to be implemented as the fabrication technique would continuously build up and lock the previous operations freezing them in time and rendering inaccessible for re-evaluation. We soon realize that this feature is crucial for allowing a

7.2

crowdsourced structure to learn and adapt as the players try and change their mind seeing what works and what doesn't. The final result of the piece, in this sense, is an extensive catalog of errors that altogether generate its particular pattern. Luckily, as soon as players started discovering the expressive power of regular sequences, other players would start imitating and generating balance in the piece.

The piece was intentionally designed symmetrically across its central vertical access, allowing the interaction to break the symmetry and generate differentiation. We hoped that the symmetry would encourage players to either adopt a 'copying' attitude, imitating patterns from one side to the other or perhaps to entirely avoid its existence, generating two sides of absolute difference. While the later was the scenario that we experience throughout the installation, the nature of the accumulative esthetic of the piece would dissolve such difference into a consistent density.

The project continues research of how game mechanics can cater for negative entropy and design outputs in the hands of its users, thinking of a future where 'prosumers' (consumers that have become producers) will challenge the role of the author and become a much stronger agency in the design process.

Assistants:

LA FABRICA (Oscar Corletto) + Alenoush Aghajanians, Anqi Yu, Arjun Mahesh, Avra Tomara, Belen Sanchez, Caroline Duncan, Guoyu Hu, JiaRui Su, Jimmie Li, Kevin Crooks, Mouna Lawrence, Olivia Tirado, Phong lee, Robbie Mehring, Sam Adelan, Setareh Ordoobadi, Vaheh Vartanian, Wu Qiong, Yueming Zhou.

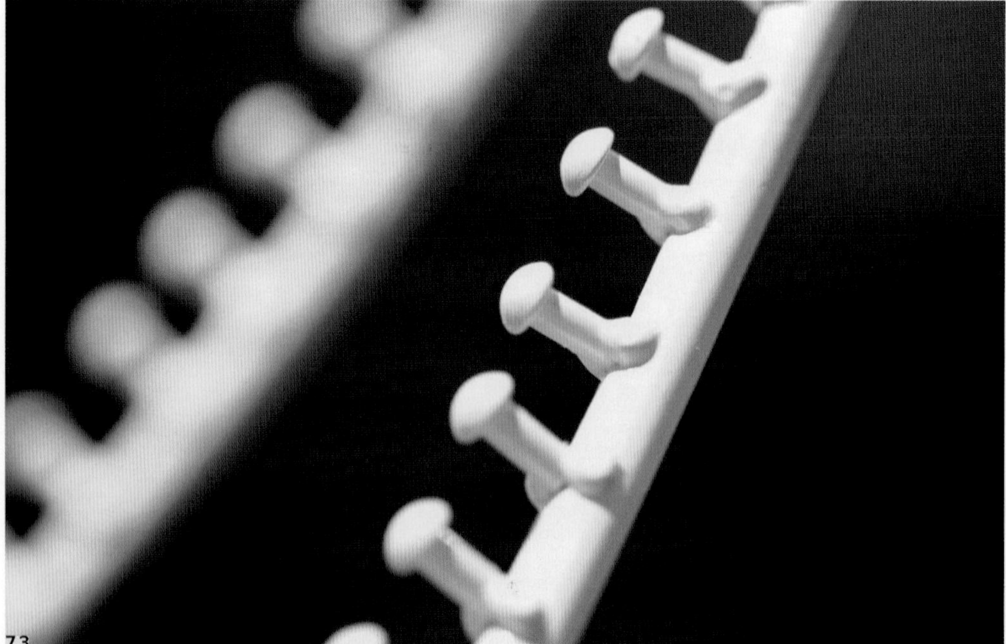
7.3

7.4

Fig. 7.1 Renders of initial concept. A fibrous construction based on crowdsourced fabrication.

Fig. 7.2 Preparation of spools for interaction.

Fig. 7.3 Detail of welded rivets in the main steel frame allowing 'players' to connect the dots with the thread. This image is before the beginning of the installation.

Fig. 7.4 Symmetrical front of the piece. The image shows the connection points between different bent steel members giving the overall shape of the project.

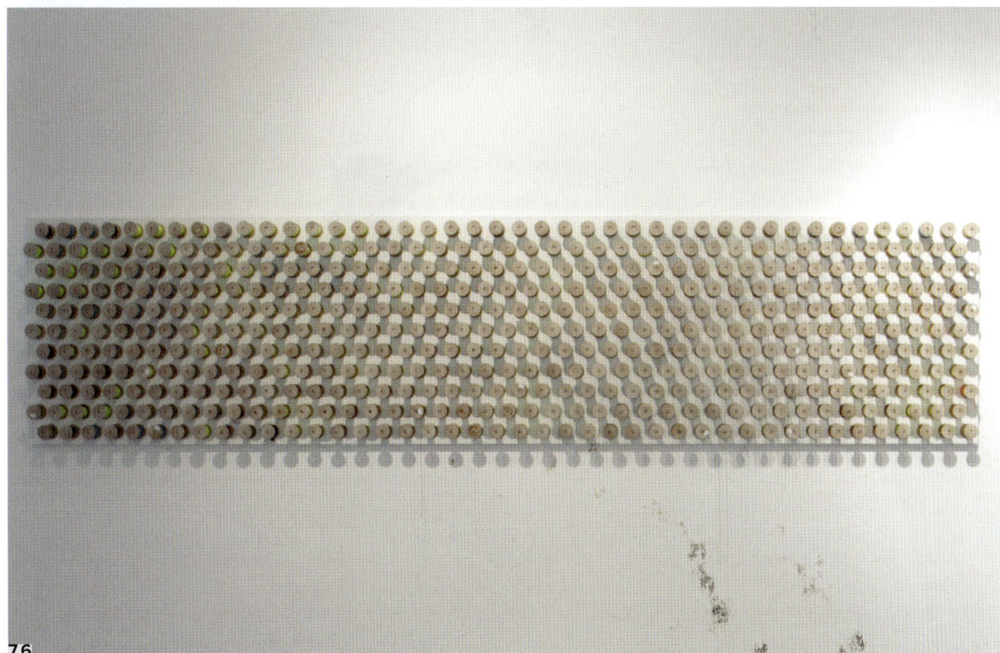

Fig. 7.5 - 7.6 Spool matrix. Presented just beside the steel structure, the spool matrix is the fundamental resource for the crowd to 'connect th e dots'. Color is presented in different porcentages, allowing for patterns to be differentiated.

Fig. 7.7 - 7.8 Crowd-source interaction. This images, taken for the opening of the piece, show the interaction of the crowd with the game.

Fig. 7.9 - 7.10 Design patterns. These images show some of the different strategies of players to connect the different steel members. The emergent surface conditions slowly kept on building density.

PRODUCT DESIGN

JENNY WU

Jenny is the founder and design director of LACE by Jenny Wu. She is also a partner at the LA-based experimental architecture firm, Oyler Wu Collaborative, which she founded in 2004 with Dwayne Oyler and the winner of 2013 Design Vanguard Award from Architectural Record. The firm is recognized for its experimentation in design, material research, and fabrication. Their recent projects include The Cube, a four-story pavilion for the Beijing Biennale as well as the design of a new 3D printing Culinary Lab in Los Angeles for 3D Systems. Wu and Oyler's success prompted Wu to start her jewelry line, LACE, upon which she places particular focus on innovative fabrication methods such as 3D printing. The intricately detailed design pieces extend from Jenny's avant-garde architectural work, merging her modern design sensibilities with the latest in 3-D printing technology and material. She is a member of the design faculty at the Southern California Institute of Architecture and recently published a new book, Trilogy, SCI-Arc Pavilions, which outlines their architectural ideas and obsessions related to line-based geometries.

I often suggest to young designers, when deciding what to study in college, to attend architecture school. While it sounds concrete, it is one of the most versatile, comprehensive design educations one can obtain. In the past ten years, I have practiced architecture with my partner, Dwayne Oyler, at the Los Angeles based firm, Oyler Wu Collaborative, and have taught architecture at SCI-Arc (Southern California Institute of Architecture). I would say that my experience as an architect has given me a distinct perspective to develop any design project whether it is large or small and from its initial design conception to final realization. Two years ago I started developing a line of 3D printed jewelry, and last year I launched the collection. The road from conception to realization was a challenging one, yet I was able to apply certain lessons from my design education to help guide me through the entire process. I have set up this introduction as a set of three questions that I would ask if I were a juror on a final review for a design project. Through these questions, I hope to reflect on my foray into product design and hope it will provide some insights to designers entering this field.

WHAT ARE YOU DESIGNING?

The answer to this question may be as simple as a product but is much stronger when it is an idea or a set of ideas. When students begin an architectural project, they often feel like they need to come up with a grand concept, one that will solve all their design issues. Coming up with an original product is not necessary about finding that comprehensive concept right from the beginning, but finding an idea that you can develop and grow with. I went into the design of my jewelry collection with two initial ideas. Each idea brings a specific angle to the design, but they can be combined with each other to create something that is better than the sum of its parts.

Initially, in thinking about the design of my collection, I was interested in creating pieces that are not singular in their function but work as hybrids. The first design for my collection, which I initially called it a "neck-dress," was a hybrid between a necklace and a collar. It works as an extension of a dress or shirt, but can still stand out on its own as a statement. This idea of the "neck-dress" helped shaped many details of the design, beginning with how the piece sits on the body to how high it comes up on the neck. I was able to develop a couple of different styles, from a "neck-dress" that looks more like a second skin to one that stands very prominently as a collar. Yet both seem to still work within the theme of this initial concept. The second idea that I wanted to implement is more qualitative than functional. I wanted the "neck-dress" to having the quality of lace, which also happens to be the name of the company. The type of lace I was interested in is less graphic but more architectural and 3-dimensional. I wanted to weave intricate elements into something that is simultaneously porous and fabric-like but still maintains its 3-dimensional and structural quality. This lace-like quality extends the line-based geometries from our architectural work to the human scale. Even as I developed and expanded the collection into designs for other parts of the body, I continued to use the idea of hybrid function to create new pieces, like a ring that is both for the finger and the knuckle.

HOW DO YOU PRODUCE IT? DO YOU NEED TO MAKE ONE OR ONE THOUSAND?

This essay is less focused on the business side of starting a new company, but it is essential to know how production and the business model can affect the creative side of the business. In fact, deciding the production method is nearly as important as designing the pieces themselves. Any student who has gone through architecture school knows that a physical model that is built in wood has as drastically different quality and production time than a 3D printed model. While knowing the end material of your product is a good starting point, the production method will dictate the quality, material limitations, and cost for your final product. To narrow down the best manufacturing method, it is essential to clarify the type of business you want to run to figure out the best way to get there.

In my case, my immediate 5-year plan is to be a small, design-oriented start-up company focusing on high-end, low-run, and well-produced pieces. With those criteria, I found 3D printing to be the best production method for this business model. In the past ten years, additive manufacturing, more commonly known as 3D printing, has made exponential advances in its technology, ranging from the variety of printable materials to scale of items that may be printed. While it is typically used for prototyping, I wanted to explore how 3D printing can be used as the primary production method. The reason for this is both out of convenience since it is a technology that architects know well and for its ability to create high-resolution products with little startup cost. The technology is such that the unit cost of printing one piece is nearly identical to the unit cost of printing a thousand pieces. Despite the fact that the production cost from 3D printing is higher than traditionally manufactured products, the benefit of 3D printing outweighs the negative, from not having to pay for a minimum order to eliminate the need to store a large quantity of inventory. These are both major considerations when working with a limited budget and limited space. Another benefit of this technology for a small start-up is that I can continuously evolve and improve my designs with every print, which is important when you are working with unconventional materials and geometries.

With that being said, this technology also has many challenges to address. The material limitation is one of the challenges. I am limited by the materials that can be produced with the technology currently available; very often those materials are inappropriate for use in my products due to required wear-ability and durability demanded by discerning consumers. The cost is another challenge that must be addressed as my business grows beyond the first five-year plan. I will need to reassess the pros and cons of this technology and whether it is evolving with the progress of the company.

NOW YOU MADE A PRODUCT, WHAT DO YOU DO NEXT?

This final topic is quite broad, and perhaps one that no design education ever quite prepares you for. I will focus on two issues: product testing and launch. I cannot emphasize enough the importance of testing your product. My schedule for launching any new item ranges from 6 to 8 months. The prototyping of the piece and perfecting the print typically takes 3 to 6 months. The main challenge is usually in the small details. In my case, the latch on the necklace was one of the most difficult elements to finalize. Each latch had to be customized to the weight and geometry of the necklace so that it had the right amount of friction to hold the latch together but still allowed the wearer to remove the necklace with some ease. Once I perfected the latch based on my own body, I spent several months sharing my work with friends and colleagues to wear as a means for receiving feedback. This provided to be an invaluable step. I realized with every unique movement of the body and slight rub of clothing against the necklace, the perfect balance that I thought I have achieved with the latch of the necklaces was thrown off. It took nearly a year before I had a latch I was happy with.

The launch of a product is a topic that one can write an entire essay about, from the business side (raising money, staffing, etc.), to distribution (stores, websites, etc.), and to marketing (branding, outreach, etc.). I would like to focus on a more conceptual discussion about how to position your product in the market and how your branding should reflect that. In my case, I knew that I wanted to build a brand that is not only at the forefront of the technology, but at the same time, create pieces can stand on their own as original, well-designed pieces. It is important to me that people appreciate the work because of its design and not merely because it is 3D printed. To elevate the brand, you have to elevate the ethos of the company by designing not just the pieces themselves, but also everything supporting it, like the packaging, website, and customer service.

Finally, knowing your audience is important not only as a design parameter but also knowing how you should market to that audience. For my line, I started by designing pieces mainly for myself, which made it easy to figure out who was in my audience. Knowing my audience helped guide product pricing, marketing, and distribution efforts. I also researched intensively brands that I felt have achieved prominence in the market and used their business strategies as a basis to direct decisions regarding my brand.

CONCLUSION

I think the biggest lesson in starting a new business is to be patient and launch your product only when you are ready. You simply cannot wholeheartedly back a product until you have done your best in creating it. Design education, perhaps, emphasizes the importance of design over any business or legal considerations. I am a real believer that good design can transcend and propel the brand to another level. The last twenty years have brought about a profound shift in the value of design, with companies from Apple to Target innovating in ways that foreground a design ethos. Good design is no longer optional; it is a necessity for survival.

ERAGATORY

ISAIE BLOCH

Isaïe Bloch is a Belgian architect and founder of Eragatory which is a creative company with a focus on design for 3D printing architecture and Creative fabrication. Isaïe's ongoing research and design ambitions are focused on the correlation between craftsmanship and Additive manufacturing within several creative domains including Architecture, Fashion and Plastic arts. Using digital tools as a new set of brushes. Currently lecturing Graduate Architectural design at the Bartlett UCL, UK; he is working under his label "Eragatory". Isaie Bloch has been collaborating with a wide range of customers and Artists, like Iris van Herpen in the design and production of 3D printed sculptures, products, and Haute Couture. His work has been shown in numerous exhibitions such as Archilab 2013 in the FRAC center Orleans Fr, SHOW cabinet London, TARP not nature NY, etc. In 2013 he won the `3d print artist of the year` award at the global 3d print show in London.

Fig.9.1 Key elements while designing the cutlery set were the notion of decay/processing, ornamental and aesthetic excess as in former Rococo and Baroque times, moments of collapse/ disequilibrium and a balance in between etiquette dining and torture tools.

9.1

BREAKING A SELF FULFILLING CYCLE

TEXT BY JOSE SANCHEZ BASED ON INTERVIEW WITH ISAIE BLOCH

Chroma is a ceramic vase conceived and developed with the aid of 3d printing techniques. The project challenges the traditional conception of 3d printing by hybridizing it with traditional forms of production; by understanding and utilizing plaster block molds and ceramic casting, the chroma project can challenge the negative preconception of digital processes.

Bloch is aware of a systemic problem in the way architects and designers conceive products; he believes we design for designers, never breaking a self-fulfilling cycle, not allowing the projects to find a larger audience. His work plays with the expectations and preconceptions of crafts & digital production, playing a conscious role in the selection of materials and the articulation of geometric features.

The work seeks to present contradictions that are articulated into a final piece; The use of smooth, elegant surfaces is juxtaposed by the addition of hi-resolution moments of detail. This comes as a challenge as well as an opportunity to develop material expressions multiple readings of the object. While the smooth surfaces have been thought with a metallic coating in mind, the more visceral detailing intends to express the pure materiality of the ceramic.

He consciously avoids the reading of a unified design 'move' as he called it. He seeks to establish a tension between different design languages, trying to stay away from any established style. The uniqueness of his pieces comes from a deep cultural awareness of the design field and the expectations from the audience. Again, thinking not in a design audience, but a consumer that could buy and use the product.

Bloch believes that the material finishes in traditional manufacturing methods exceed the possibilities of current 3D printing technologies, so he intelligently positions 3D printing as part of the manufacturing process, and not as a final product. The 3D printed prototype defines the external geometry out of which a plaster block mold is created. This is used for the ceramic slip casting. The result, although initiated with digital techniques, allows for a material differentiation of each of the pieces, where physics play a role in the detail and overall expression of the piece.

'It is not enough to do a 3d printed prototype' claims Bloch, encouraging designers to pursue the development of a product as a business opportunity that could find an audience. He is aware of the different impact that a digital image could have vs. the power of showing a product cast in metal. He believes that it is still an important interested for crafted products and that 'the digital' suffers from lesser value.

This was key for the development of the cutlery set; what was initially a niche piece with a small success, was transformed into a mass market opportunity once the first metal cast pieces started being developed. Bloch reflects on the different audience and clients at different stages of development and understands the value to give a sense of 'reality' to the product. This reality comes with his craft and material finishes that make his pieces stand out in a global catalog.

Bloch sees a design chain that starts with rapid prototyping moving towards a small high-end market, one in which the work can be exhibited and find an audience to finally hit mass production reconsidering some material attributes. He sees the value of access, not rejecting the idea of one of his products to end up in the Ikea catalog.

9.2

Hi thinks designers should go deeper into the understanding of distribution and how it can influence the design process.

Bloch, with his firm, Eragatory, has started developing a formula to break the dichotomy between analog and digital, and leaving that conversation as a thing of the past. His fluidity between digital craftsmanship and material expression describe a more seamless transition between current and future forms of production.

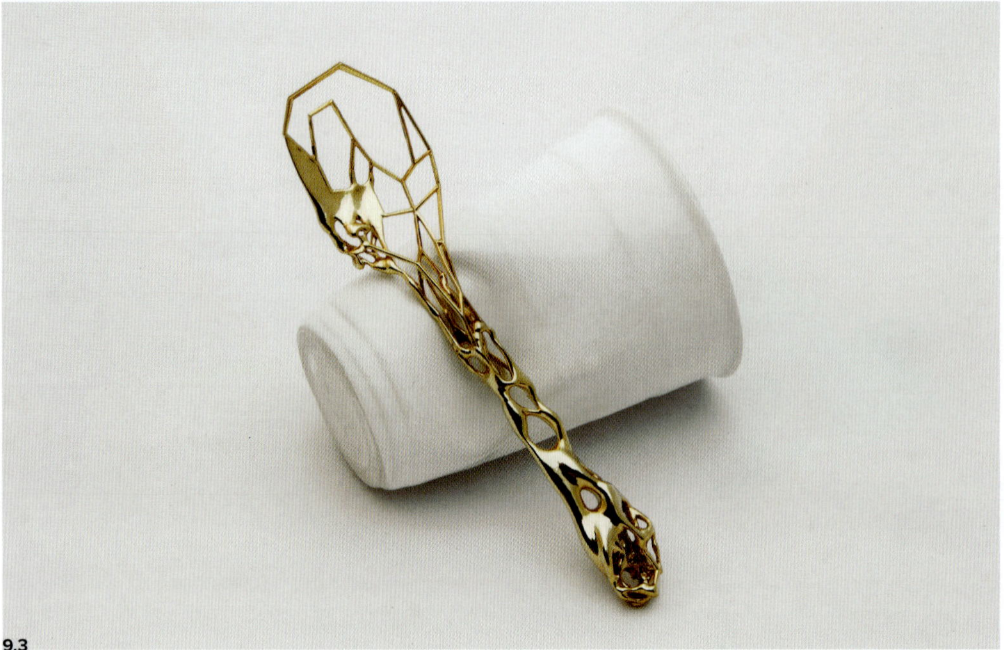

9.3

9.4

Fig. 9.2 Considering the reduced definition after glazing ceramics, the Chroma series of vases investigates the degree of ornamental saturation which can endure the potential loss in detailing or uneven distribution of the glaze while keeping its specific overall aesthetics.

Fig. 9.3-9.5 By subverting the logic of perfection and beauty, non-perfect images coming from controlled methodologies were generated. What used to be about mastering the result of a non-perfect process is now about the production of monstrosity and the grotesque throughout very accurate mechanisms, like 3d printing. Which creates an unlimited range of possibilities concerning material usage, design approaches/aesthetics, and form production.

Dim: Fork - 26 * 187 * 16 mm
Spoon - 42 * 188 * 17 mm
Thee spoon - 30 * 137 * 13 mm
Knife - 29 * 219 * 14 mm

Medium: 3D printed lost wax cast -Brass or 925 Sterling Silver

Archilab 2013: Naturalizing Architecture, Les Turbulences FRAC Centre – Orléans, Fr

SHOWcabinet: Iris van Herpen, SHOWstudio – London, GB

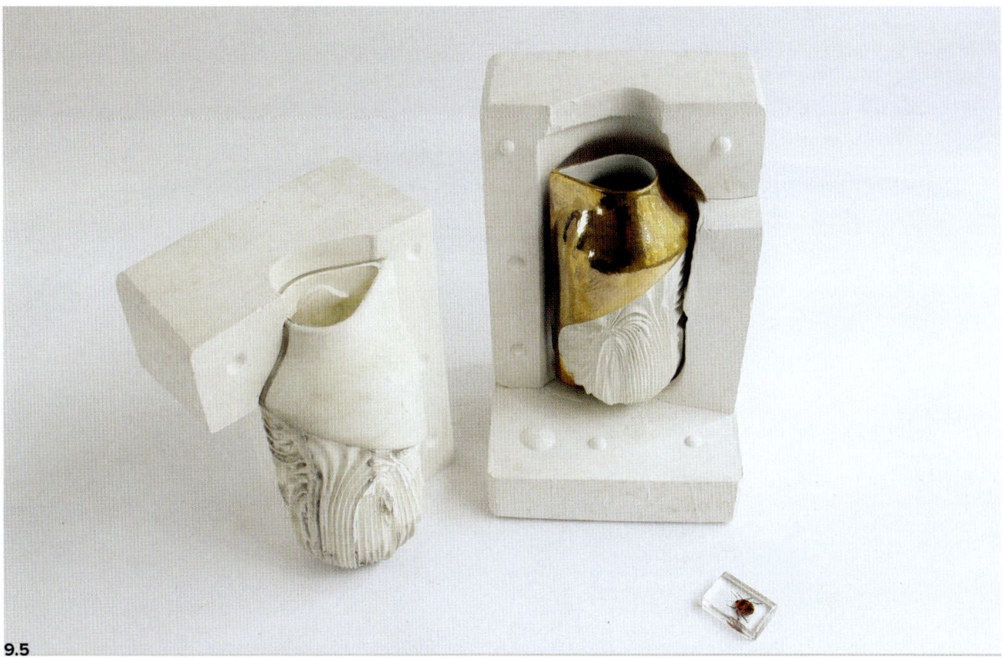

9.5

9.6

Fig. 9.6-9.7 The delicate juxtaposition of the slick outer shell and its rougher tactile ornated canister combines best of both worlds regarding what ceramic 3d printers can achieve.

Dim: Cement - 140 * 140 * 280 mm
Polyamide – 250 * 250 * 500 mm
Medium: 3D printed ceramic, 3D printed cement polymer, 3D printed SLS polyamide

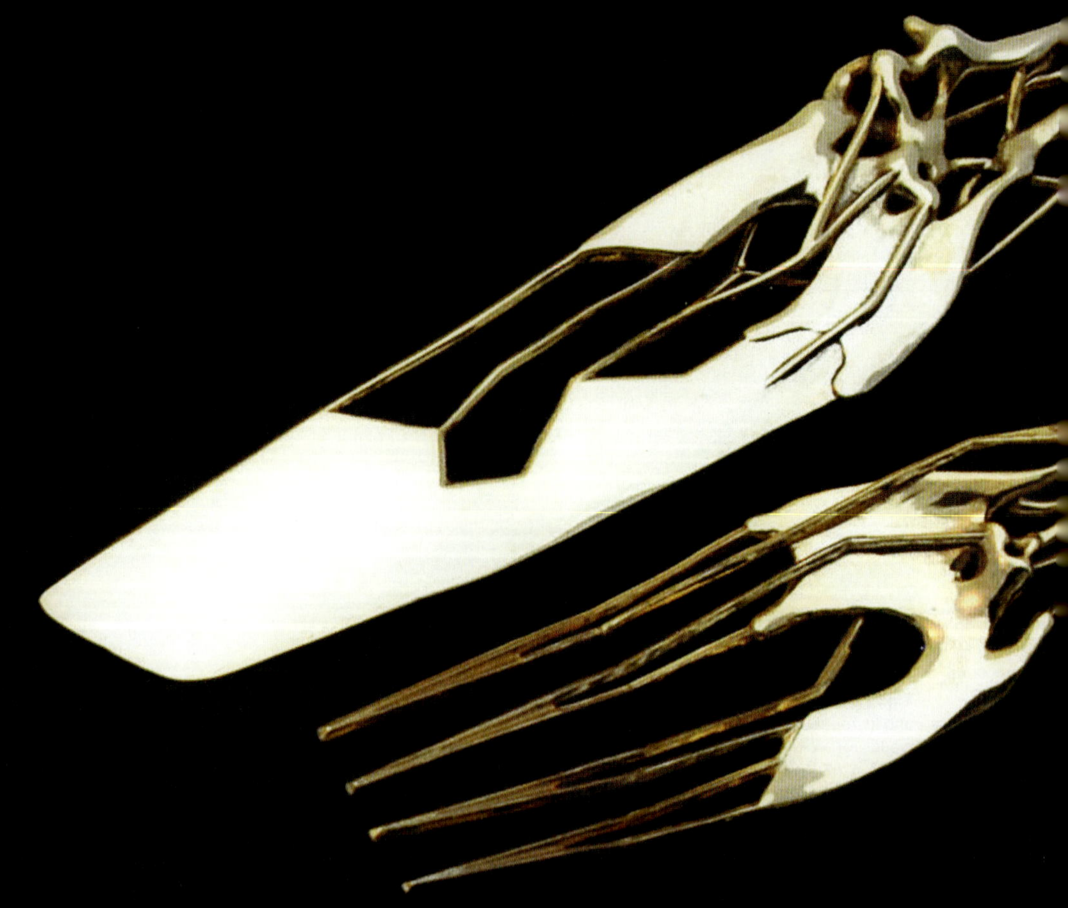

9.7

NICCOLO CASAS

Italian architect and professor Niccolo Casas is currently a Ph.D. candidate at The Bartlett UCL London and a faculty member at RISD - Rhode Island School of Design.

Inspired by entropy phenomena that cause the design to arise and evolve in nature as patterns, his work aspires to capture beauty in its mutable state and inevitable decline.
His research highlights the convergence of architecture, art, and fashion design via the application of emergent digital technologies and additive manufacturing.

His most recent works include the collaboration on additive manufactured pieces with 3D printing company 3D System, and fashion designer Iris Van Herpen for the Magnetic Motion and Hacking Infinity haute couture shows and for "The future of fashion is now" exhibition at the Museum Boijmans Van Beuningen in Rotterdam.

10.1

BLACK TURBULENCE

Black Turbulence is a necklace designed by the Italian architect Niccolo Casas in partnership with the Spanish fashion designer Leyre Valiente, and 3D printed by the additive manufacturing company Materialise in 2013.

It is part of a two pieces collaboration -Turbulence and Black Turbulence- presented at the Mercedes Benz Fashion Week in Madrid in March 2013 and part of the Leyre Valiente collection, “Malleus Maleficarum”.

Black Turbulence results from the process of investigation on Catabiosis, Entropy, and Decadence that Niccolo Casas is researching through his Ph.D. at The Bartlett in London.

Catabiosis is the process of aging, senescence and physical degradation. It comes from the Greek word “Kata” - down, against, reverse, and “Biosis” - a way of life. It is used to describe processes that are apparently different such as human aging, plant senescence, and object decay.

All spontaneous happenings in the animate or inanimate world involve energy dispersing, all of the minute particles, the atoms or molecules, are in constant violent random motion[1] and they naturally tend to spread out their motional energy. This spontaneous energy dispersal of molecular motional energy in space, the force working against life, that Greeks called catabiosis, is in fact entropy.

Entropy from the Greek en = in + trope = a turning (point) is a term coined by physicist Rudolf Clausius[2] in 1865, it is “the measure of a system's thermal energy per unit temperature that is unavailable for doing useful work”[3], in other words, the degree of degradation of energy.

All the patterns, configurations and rhythms we see in nature arise thanks to entropy phenomena; they emerge from the continuous battle between the tendency toward equilibrium and the constant support of energy from the sun.

The term ‘Turbulence’ in fact refers to the tendency in nature to equilibrate not only the hot with the cold but also the fast with the slow, generating movement and irregular transitions between laminar and turbulent flows.

If Catabiosis is the process and Entropy is the physical law that drives it, Decadence is the artistic reinterpretation of it: Decadent beauty is a catabiotic beauty: beauty at the moment it starts to crumble, announcing its inevitable decline.

The term entropy was in fact coined for the first time in 1865 just a few years before the publication of Les Fleurs du Mal. Thus, it gave birth to (or at least scientifically supported) the pessimistic mood of the late nineteenth and the beginning of the twentieth century[4]. The sober formulations of Clausius before, and Kelvin[5] and Boltzmann[6] later, became proofs and demonstrations of the underlying cause of the gradual decay of all things physical and mental[7].

This gave birth to what was later defined by Paul Bourget[8] as “le style de la Décadence”: the style of Decadence[9].

Decadence was described by Paul Bourget as a process of decomposition of an organism (human and social) that enables the cell to be freed from the hierarchy and subordination of the whole:

Decadence is a process of entropy increase: the disintegration of the whole where the particular gains autonomy and incrementation of visibility by shirking from the functional subordination of the whole. If we consider Decadence as a state of dynamic transition leading to the fragmentation of the whole, it is the Fractal geometry that articulates this process: fractal geometries emerge analogically and optimally from the thermodynamic tendency toward equilibrium, resulting from the way nature deterministically

10.2

breaks symmetry while minimizing energy waste for the principle of least action.

Black Turbulence is about the simulation of a fractured system in which the whole decomposes making singularities emerge, it concerns the process of fragmentation of a system of relations, and it is the expression of the corrupted complexity generated by simple iterations.

Fractals are an infinite process of self-similar repetition. They are theoretically endless shapes that only computers can calculate, even if their precision is linked to the power of the processors and the time of rendering that becomes the time of generation.

In consequence, the process of 3D mesh extrapolation is extremely complex; this process can take anywhere from minutes to hours, depending on the complexity of the fractal set.

Once the object has been calculated, the mesh must then be exported, and polygon optimization methods must be applied since the generated meshes tend to be incredibly dense and it is not uncommon for many of these objects to be more than 1-3 million polygon faces.

10.3

Fig. 10.1-10.2 Black Turbulence, 3d printed necklace by Niccolo Casas and Leyre Valiente was recently photographed by Luca Piras. The necklace is part of a two pieces collaboration - Turbulence and Black Turbulence - presented at the Mercedes Benz Fashion Week in Madrid in March 2013 and part of the Leyre Valiente collection, "Malleus Maleficarum".

Fig. 10.3 Turbulence is about the simulation of a fractured system in which the whole decomposes making singularities emerge, it concerns the process of fragmentation of a system of relations, and it is the expression of the corrupted complexity generated by simple iterations.

In the Black Turbulence piece, the outcomes of the fractal simulation were eventually organized and distributed as components along the body and around the neck of a 3d scanned model resulting in a symmetric organization.

Mario Carpo in "Breaking the curve: big data and design" displays how a disconnected, broken, fragmentary aesthetic results from the evolution of digital computation; Black Turbulence designed by Niccolo Casas and Leyre Valiant is a perfect example of this tendency.

[1] Oxygen molecules in our air, on average, are moving about a thousand miles an hour at ordinary temperatures, but changing from 0 to almost 3000 miles an hour as they crash into other molecules after moving about 15 millionths of an inch. In solids, the particles 'dance in place' (vibrate) with energies dependent on temperature.

[2] Rudolf Clausius, in full Rudolf Julius Emanuel Clausius (1822-1888), German mathematical physicist who formulated the second law of thermodynamics and is credited with making thermodynamics a science. Source Encyclopedia Britannica

[3] Source Encyclopedia Britannica

[4] "Thermodynamics and History: Science and Culture in the 19th century." The Graduate Journal, 7; 1967. pp. 477-565.

[5] Lord Kelvin (Willliam Thomson) In 1851 expressed the second law as: "It is impossible, by means of inanimate material agency, to derive mechanical effect from any portion of matter by cooling it below the temperature of the coldest of the surrounding objects"

[6] Boltzmann formula (1872) shows the relationship between entropy and the number of ways the atoms or molecules of a thermodynamic system can be arranged. Boltzmann links entropy to statistical mechanics.

[7] Psychoanalysis starts at the end of nineteens century: in 1886 Freud first began providing therapy.

[8] Paul Bourget (1852-1935) was a french novelist and critic

[9] Bourget P. Edited by Francesca Manno. Décadence Saggi di psicologia contemporanea. Torino, Italia: Nino Aragno Editore; 2007.

10.4

10.5

Fig. 10.4-10.5 The outcomes of the fractal simulation are eventually organized and distributed as component in an "extreme symmetric system" (as symmetry of animated and dynamic components).

10.6

Fig. 10.6-10.8 Black Turbulence is the second necklace generated via fractal system simulations and designed with the Spanish fashion designer Leyre Valiente and presented at the London 3D Printshow 2013. It pushes the boundaries of the research on "extreme symmetric conditions" that started with the "white" Turbulence, by introducing a second piece that is the twin of the first one. The basic equation that describes the general dynamical system, using complex number - Z(n+1) = Zn2 +C - remained the same for the white and black turbulence whereas the parameters related to the component data and their overall symmetric disposition changed radically.

Blindspot Initiative

10.7

10.8

WILL HOSIKIAN

Will Hosikian the Melbourne born architect and designer leads a double life. By day he is Principal and Design Director for architecture at Woods Bagot in Beijing, but there is another side to Hosikian that will be unveiled soon, in parallel he will be launching WillHosikian.com, a collection of personal research projects exploring the nexus between architecture, technology, and digital design, with a specific focus on Product & industrial design for film.
His recent appointment as Principal at Woods Bagot is quite an accomplishment for the 31-year-old as the youngest partner in the organization's history. Hosikian holds a Master of Architecture from of RMIT University, where he also received the Antonia Brunz thesis prize. He also holds a Bachelor of Design- Architecture from Deakin University with a focus on building construction, a Bachelor of Interior Architecture with Honours from Monash University in Melbourne where he was also a thesis prize recipient.

Will has undertaken research studios at the Southern California Institute of Architecture in Los Angeles (SCI-ARC) for the X-treme studio, exploring zero gravity space habitation. In 2008 also attending Urban strategies at the Angewandte in Vienna, as well as the Architectural Association Rovinj Global School. With a focus on leading some of Woods Bagots most notable recent globally-significant competition projects.

SPECULATIVE FUTURISM

The design work of Will Hosikian is heavily influenced by product design, industrial design illustration, furniture de-sign, and fabrication. While trained as an architect, most of his early work was interdisciplinary. The progressive crossover with different disciplines developed a sense of ambition in Hosikian's work challenging scales and subjects in an attempt to expand to new territories.

The convergence of design disciplines, has blurred the boundaries between traditional design discourses, catalyzed as the digital tools although specialized, have become more accessible, bridging conventional borders of practice between digital media, architecture, product, industrial and automotive design.

It is only through the paradigm of design that one can explore the potentials of another imagined futurism. Future trends determined by social, political, environmental and technological shifts acting together as a time-based catalyst for design speculation.
Let's not confuse this with science fiction, exploring Futurism is in the shifting and friction between these interactions which give rise to the emergence of new functional, spatial, sensorial, material, structural implications, which formalize into new potential design outcomes for the real world.

Understanding designer's role, not as material scientists or politicians, the humanistic needs, and tendencies, coupled with the desire for change, have empowered an understanding of technological advancement. With the exponential rise of automated rapid prototyping and manufacturing at an incrementally more finite resolution, conceptually exploiting material systems and structural limitations become just as equally malleable as sub divisional modeling techniques. It is in this unknown and often naïve territory between the real world, and the digital that gives us license to create new sensibilities both functionally and aesthetically.

Speculative futurism in digital design, product or architecture is not just about visual provocation; it is a test bed where we ponder fundamental human questions, re-imagining the necessities of future human habitation, products, transportation and associated network systems. This, in turn, forms a feedback loop as our work collectively influences the trajectory of future technology trends as we strive to engineer our unfettered creativity into the real world.

How one navigate these new territories, researching parallel disciplines, responding to new criteria for space, form, and function hypothetically, and speculate with a tangibility, especially while we see continued exponential movement in technological, is what drives Hosikian's multiscalar design inquiry.

"A further dimension and a more interesting one personally to test the limits of a designer, is the understanding of an object at a specific time. In the back of your mind, time shifts becoming a much more powerful catalyst for design speculation. "

TheSDX 1 concept car project is a cross hybrid supercar with self-drive capabilities. The project started imagining a designer set 30 or more years from now, where the self-drive technologies are standard in transportation design, and urban infrastructures in place to facilitate their deployment, but also paying homage to the elements of a present-day supercar, merging elements forward in time as a retrospective concept, an exploration into both new aesthetics, functionality, and materiality.

11.2

11.3

Fig. 11.1 Top view of the SDX 1 concept car, a continuous glass surface exposing the interior. The glass is pleated in areas to re-emphasize the directionality and lines of the body, also providing strength in material where stress naturally occurs. The transparent engine cover is exposing the drive mechanics of the rear wheel base.

Fig. 11.2-11.3 Front and top view. A wireframe transition between surface geometry and the engineered mechanical inner workings, highlighting the air intakes to the front left and right, forward of the concealed wheel base to provide airflow.

11.4

11.5

Fig. 11.4-11.5 The scissor doors seamlessly disengage the body, lifting up to its open position, the forward edge hovering parallel to the ground. The curved glass profile a continuation of the vehicle body. All lines are flowing from its front to rear profile defining the door and wheel surface enclosure. The rear wheel profile is held by a series of carbon fiber air intakes to cool the concealed wheel base.

Fig. 11.6-11.7 The interior, a two seater cabin, comprised of a carbon fiber inner shell, sculpted to be reminiscent of classic luxury supercars combining leather with two details of carbon fiber and the digital interfaces. The dashboard comprises of 3 tiers, 1) between driver and passenger self-drive, power, comfort controls. 2) Above, the navigational display 3) upper heads-up display, vehicle systems, speed, and proximity.

Aesthetically, the traditional engender an industrial product or object with either masculine or feminine line, exploring the middle ground, blurring the perceivable boundary between the two is often where intuitively the final formal iteration resides. This largely subconscious process often informs the incremental push and pull of surface subdivisions and overall formal topology. Essentiality a relentless iterative formal exploration driven by an intuitive satisfaction.

We will see a drastic shift in the overall shape of vehicle design for more than just aesthetic reasons, the most re-cent to occur will be a result of the autonomous self-drive capabilities as they make transportation safer, pedestrian impact zones at the front of the vehicles will be reduced bringing forward the front wheelbase to the nose.

Concealing the wheels was a key feature in the exterior styling as it represents what I consider to feel autonomous. However, the wheel locations are referenced in the surface language and part line assembly.

The exterior wing doors seamlessly disengage the main body and rotate out and up exposing the detailed carbon fiber, chrome and leather interior with digital HUD interface. The interior is detailing also reminiscent of classic supercar interiors.

The dashboard and HUD becomes a full self-drive navigation display. It is also symmetrical in design so the manual steering mechanism can be disengaged and folded away, or switch for both left and right-hand driving as desired. The windscreen also becomes an extension of the digital dashboard as an augmented reality extension of the HUD.
The rear is complete with a fully integrated finite led display which acts as the vehicles indicators, stop light and any programmable graphic theming as desired. The fine LED nodes a direct vertex extraction and illumination of original sub divisional topology.

The rear engine becomes visually exposed at the touch of a button through a polycarbonate liquid crystal film composite that when charged varies opacity accordingly. This further accentuates the singular overall slender surface of the concept while concealing its underlying mechanics. Although the engine is rear mounted, the air intakes to the front of the vehicle supply flow to the concealed wheelbase.

The surface construction and material are a new Aluminium Alloy AlSi10Mg, a new 3d printing material that will revolutionize the aerospace and automotive industry. It will be one of the lightest and strongest metals available. Graphene being extruded within thermoplastics another potential material system we will see emerging, which has its unique benefits. However a more left of field bio-derived material currently in development that will further transform the automotive and manufacturing industries are Nanocellulose reinforced polymers which pose a complete evolution in material sciences for manufacturing. As this new material derived from ultra-strong naturally occurring nanoparticles, has a comparable strength ratio to current carbon fiber reinforced structures, with a much lighter composition and cost. Combined with such automated prototyping concepts as the (BAAM) Big Area Additive Manufacturing 3d printer, we will see our unfettered creativity come to fruition sustainably and very quickly at full scale.

Eventually, user defined customization will have to come into play; you could assemble from a pre-designed kit of virtual parts, your personalized versions of transportation design, which would be quickly deployable from a local micro-

11.8

Fig. 11.8-11.9 The rear is complete with a fully integrated finite led display which acts as the vehicles indicators, stop light and any programmable graphic theming as desired. The fine LED nodes a direct vertex extraction and illumination of original subdivisional topology.
The rear engine becomes visually exposed at the touch of a button through a polycarbonate liquid crystal film composite that when charged varies opacity accordingly. This further accentuates the singular overall slender surface of the concept while concealing its underlying mechanics.

factory and be on the road within 24 hrs. As the materials are recyclable, after some years you could sell it back to the manufacturer who would melt components back to their original state, have a portion of the original cost re-credited, or use the recycled material towards your next upgrade. With design disciplines and material sciences working together we can facilitate the desire to change for a more sustainable and progressive future before a more immanent precibus of change will be required of us.

11.9

FILM

KATE DAVIES

Kate Davies is an artist, architect, and writer. She is deeply interested in how people inhabit and understand the landscape, particularly those places that are extreme, hostile or remote. She has undertaken expeditions to remote parts of the globe; from far North Alaska to the Australian outback; the Indian Himalayas, the Chernobyl Exclusion Zone, and the Canadian wilds. Her work explores contemporary notions of wilderness - drawing on modes of understanding landscape ranging from contemporary survey technologies to folklore - and operates between writing, drawing, film, and photography.

The combination of moving image, spoken word, text, and music – plus the way that combination shoots like a needle straight into the cerebral cortex – makes the movie the most powerful and compelling text we have yet created."
Stephen Apkon

I am watching a film on my phone, on the 97 bus. It was made by a teenager; shot on his phone, edited in a bedroom halfway across the world and uploaded yesterday. It has no dialog, and yet it communicates deftly and articulately, and in the space behind my eyes it opens up a world, 25 images a second, every second. This movie - a packet of time 5mins 38 seconds long - is just a single particle in the vast intoxicating miasma of moving images we breathe in and breathe out every day. Inhale; war, cute cat, advert, art. Exhale; my face, my meal, my cat, my art - my fragmentary biopic. Watch this incredible thing halfway, or that beautiful thing to the end. Here, amusing junk. There, a call to arms. Collectively breathing in [200 million hours of content watched every day] and breathing out [300 hours uploaded every minute.].

In the lucid dreams of play, pause, and replay, the moving image is the global vernacular, a dialect we are all naturally fluent in and the wealthiest text we have yet created. I can communicate without words, with just an emailed link. Like handing someone a mint, or a note in class, or a piece of my mind in silence. You know what to do with it [Click] and out of the [underlined] blue, a stream of moving images direct to synapses.

Our eyes take us places, slipping across the permeable membranes of liquid crystal, into territories of the screen worlds beyond, and with them flow architectural concerns, spatial tactics, social, cultural political and technical convergences - all human life is in the 'here-there' of these screen worlds. They are a simultaneous space of communication and inhabitation both territory and billboard. We live here surfing, socializing and searching. We know this. The average 8-year-old spends 8 hours a day staring at pixels - tractor beams on those naked little eyes - and perhaps we sometimes wish it wasn't so but we are conditioned by the environments we occupy, and this is a world we squarely inhabit.

We the native speakers of the moving image have been wandering around in them all our lives, powerfully literate at reading them, tutored in grammar by Kubrick, Scorsese, and Hitchcock [of course]; and in turn by Hollywood schmaltz, EastEnders Scooby Doo and Coco-Pops ads alike. Making films was once like painting in gold out of our reach but through the radical democratization of the tools of creating them, we have all been given the power to the author. The power of that liquid light elixir, once restricted to big-budget studios, is now flowing from bedroom studios across the world and where once we merely adored listeners, we now have the facilities to speak this mother tongue And what a visceral, immersive tongue it is adept at simultaneously evoking the actual and the imagined, as our communications draw ever closer to the flavor of a thought. Everyone is promoted to storyteller, with this mash of cinema, TV, YouTube, video games, moving billboards and gif memes as our giant oral lore. Moving images mediate our understanding of the world both reflecting reality and reinventing it, conjuring powerful and convincing narratives. And here in this turbulent sea of verbs is an important, exciting emerging site, ripe for tactical intervention.

Of course, architecture and cinema have enjoyed a long and well-documented love affair – soul-mates from two different tribes. Film adored architecture and architecture adored film, but these black and white archi-film romances were just an elegant prequel to the wild orgy and illegitimate offspring of current disciplinary transgressions. Quite suddenly the full power of the moving image has entered the realms of hacker culture, in a way that invites creative tinkerers to play, mixing new and potent cocktails in the chemistry set of the bedroom studio and inducing work that teeters in the space between representation and direct experience.

In the year that saw Sundance premiere a film shot entirely on an iPhone, the power of the tools available now puts students squarely on par with professional realms of cinema, television, and advertising. What we are talking about here is not purely photographic. These are not whimsical forays into art-house cinema; they go beyond the brooding narrative show-reels of film school. What architecture students are doing with the moving image vernacular is the very kind of mash-up of media for which architecture school studios seem to be magnificently fertile incubators. Design students now have wildly sophisticated means at their fingertips with which to visualize ideas, to construct and understand complex thoughts intuitively and communicate them viscerally. With cinema quality cameras, CGI, 3d modeling, VFX software, game engines, 3d imaging and scanning technologies within easy reach, the site of representation has exploded and, architectural or otherwise, it is taking on a force and power that makes it more than ever a site in itself. Paper architecture or more appropriately, pixel architecture becomes an inhabitable extension of built architecture and our task as designers is to reassess the tools of the discipline in the light of this shift.

Film is a fluid, flowing in light, of itself somewhat anti-material, anti-tectonic, far from the nature of built architecture one might say. Architects making films? Shouldn't this of all disciplines stay rooted in the physical realm? Perhaps, but one of architectures most critical practices is the prototyping of reality, to plant the seeds of possibility and bring something that has never existed into being in someone else's mind. The [architectural] drawing which has always been our virtual realm has simply grown up - come of age. We are stepping into our drawings, living them, trying them on for size. We are inviting others to join us and to occupy our ideas through the moving image, in search of direct communication, imagination to imagination. And by launching into the continuum of time, we launch headlong into prototyping of potential realities. The drawing, the 'representational site' has swung open its doors and become a public space. A site that truly approaches the complexity of the things it represents.

As the ultimate plastic, a timeline works peculiarly and magically as a design tool, engendering patterns of thinking about space that is quite distinct from the static compositional games of architectural formalism. It's a mode of design thinking that is relational, temporal and choreographic. Operating in flux rather than stasis, embracing multiplicity and action over the singular and the passive and breathing life into matter. It holds ambiguity in its temporal folds and slips into the spaces between things, stitching together disparate locations and timeframes, building spatial narratives like surgical operations. In the heady throws of the moving image, the act of design becomes a performance, which 'practices space and prototypes occupation. In the furnaces of these timelines, fuelled by exponential leaps in computational power, alternate worlds materialize unbeholden to gravity. Streams of light caught by lenses are mixed in pixel-shifting alchemy with the computer rendered and the data-driven. Here high-definition, melt in the mouth footage fuses with the digital gymnastics of CGI, motion graphics and virtual cinematography, so that in-camera and post-production become twin spaces for the creative manipulation of reality. This is the construction of thick texts, indexical hallucinations, and poetic data-scapes, as the photo-real dissolves into wild fusions of cartographic, info-graphic and typographic noodling.

So here are these visual tools, direct-to-audience, ripe for co-opting. The danger, of course, is that the skill and deftness, the smart adaptability and the seductive visuals created by these young talents are so hungrily and readily co-opted by the very commercial mechanisms we should all be seeking to re-appropriate. And here I make a gentle plea: Be aware of what your work is selling and keep an eye on the things you argued for in those coffee-fueled crit rooms of your education. Graduating students should emerge, blinking into the light, not asking for someone to find their talents useful but to forge the usefulness themselves, to invent it. And in the following pages this is what you will find, young designers engaging in a deep questioning of the nature of practice, interrogating the edges and like Darwin's finches, finding ecological niches - Infiltrating the powerful aesthetic territories previously held out of their reach by behemoths of entertainment and advertising.

These may be our architectural battlegrounds, seemingly far from the heartland, but waging a war that may be critical to that heartland nonetheless. To make your case, you need not build. We know this from the rich wealth of speculative architectural works we pored over as students. There are no real hard distinctions between disciplines, there is always an unsteady shoreline to walk upon, the edges of the manicured lawn where the weeds grow - out of place.

In these pages, between this stream of words, moving images will exist in substitute, as embalmed stills plucked from their streams of time. Films will be described in text, and as such will be the ghosts of the thing they represent, like clumsily translated proverbs. The thing that makes them what they are will be absent, they will not move, and so, perhaps they will not move you. To exist within the image-video fest that punctuates our every day is to operate on a living brain. Make no mistake, the designers you will encounter on the pages that follow, are not engaging in some niche or peripheral pursuit, they are busy mainlining the bloodstream of a global culture.

UNIVERSAL ASSEMBLY UNIT

WILLIAM GOWLAND
OLIVIU LUGOJAN GHENCIU
SAMANTHA LEE
ZHAN WANG

Universal Assembly Unit is a multi-disciplinary London based studio, working at the intersection of art, technology, and culture.

Through self-initiated and commissioned projects, the studio explores dynamic spatial design and virtual environments. Their output encompasses a diverse variety of mediums including multi-platform design, digital interactive experiences, physical installation, animation, and audio/visual performance.

12.1

DATUM EXPLORER

Datum Explorer is a multi-platform project, documenting and exploring the habitation of digital environments. With ever more powerful operating environments capable of running complex simulated worlds in real time, the immersion into virtual reality becomes increasingly pervasive. As a design territory, it presents a blank canvas which is occupied through various techniques of digitization of the real world. In this context, the world becomes a resource of potential 3D assets to be re-imagined in the next shooter game, featuring zombies and realistic bullet ballistics.

Positioned in a cultural context outside of the gaming industry, Datum Explorer questions our role as architects and designers to inhabit these virtual worlds and searches for opportunities to connect us back to the real world. With the ability to access these virtual sites across numerous devices, the project addresses the changing nature of space across desktops, mobiles, and site-specific installation.

Datum Explorer is constructed from 3D laser scans of woodlands in East Sussex. We chose to digitize a natural environment to question how we might explore a digital wilderness in the same contemplative mindset as a real physical landscape. A terrestrial LiDAR scanner was used to capture the physical environment in minute detail as a dense coloured point cloud. Left exposed in its raw state the point cloud becomes the ethereal backdrop of a new aesthetic of nature.

In parallel, we used a binaural microphone to record the rich soundscape in 3D stereo sound. The site was methodically surveyed, moving the position of the scanner and microphone in exact locations to create an overlapping three-dimensional data set of geometry, texture, and sound. Finally, this dataset was combined with a real-time engine to create an exploratory digital woodland, part site survey and part game environment filled with elusive animals.

For a temporary installation, the digital game was taken back to the original woods, projecting the virtual world into the real physical one. The installation appears as a constructed 'data atmosphere', illuminated against the dark forest backdrop. A temporary architecture in which visitors dissolve into the flickering point cloud and collectively discover the space. Here the physical environment becomes a screen, and the pixels become the grains of reality. This is brought to life by the ghostly appearances of simulated animals, disappearing and reappearing in response to visitor's movement. Each animal emits a unique digitally augmented sound, creating a continually changing soundscape as you move through the site.

The project exists across multiple platforms, in which the same virtual environment is experienced differently depending on how you view it. The mobile app is connected to the physical world though a geo-locative trigger - if someone returns to the original site with a smartphone, the virtual forest playfully explodes into a seasonal bloom.

These multiple scenarios demonstrate ways we may experience real-world datasets through digital storytelling. Despite digital media's bad reputation for gluing us to our screens, it can also be used to reveal hidden narrative layers that enrich our sense of reality and render the familiar into an exotic space.

12.2

Fig. 12.1 Datum Explorer is a multi-platform project, documenting and exploring the inhabitation of digital environments. It is both an app and a site-specific installation.

Fig. 12.2 The point cloud was projected back into its original environment to create an immersive experience fusing nature and data.

Fig. 12.3 – 12.4 Original site and point cloud visualization based on Lidar technology.

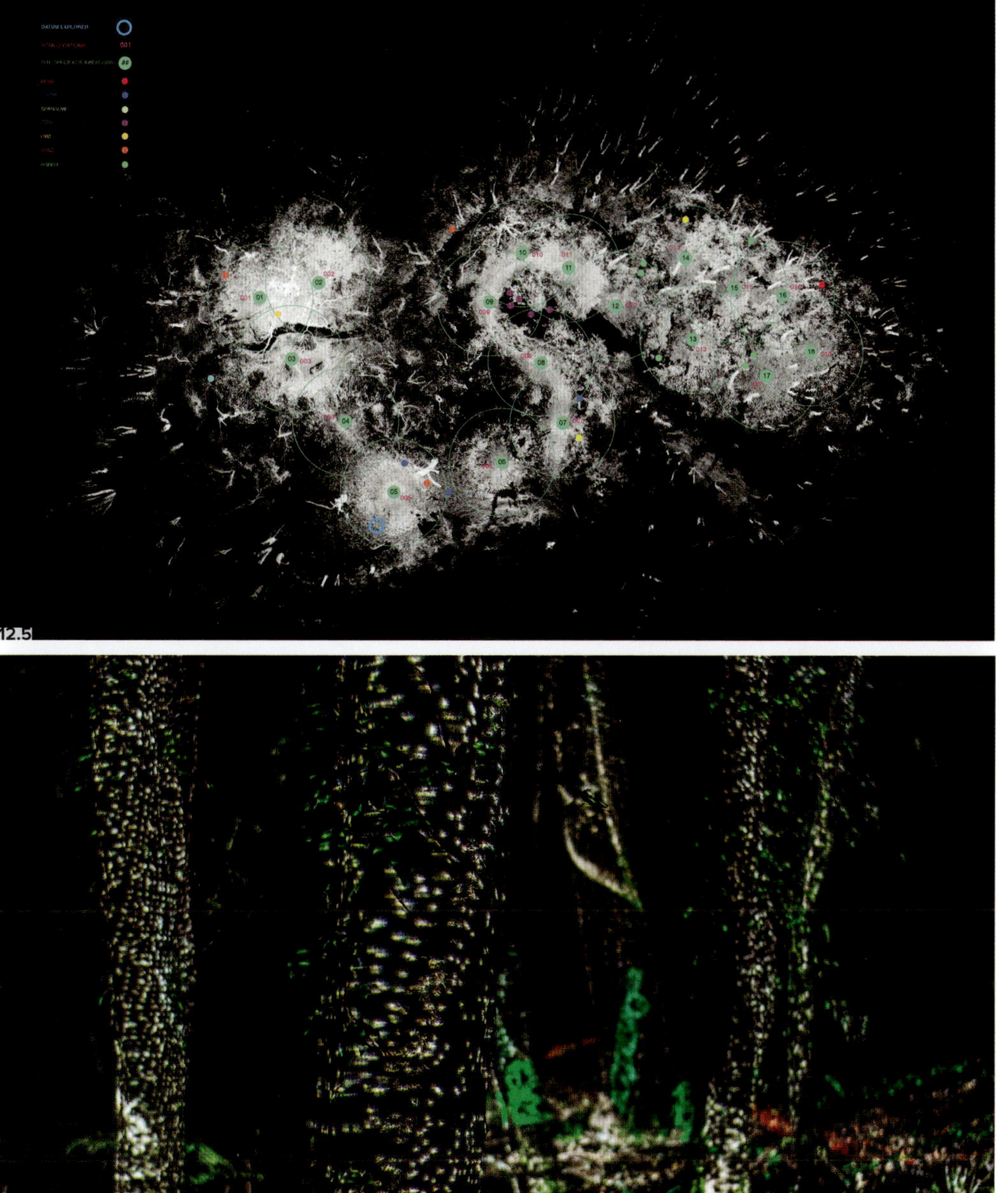

Fig. 12.5 Plan of the site with projection and lidar collection points.

Fig. 12.6 – 12.7 Close up of hybrid visualization technique combining 3D point cloud with actual location.

12.7

Blindspot Initiative

ISOHALE

CATHERINE GRIFFITHS

Catherine Griffiths works at the intersection of design, computation, and future cinema. Her research focuses on the visualization of algorithms, in the context of machine learning and the ethics of algorithms debate.

She is the principal at Isohale a design studio working with new technologies and creative code to develop cinematic visualizations of scientific data and environmental processes. Previously, she worked for architecture and engineering firms on design visualization and pilot studies for coastal technology projects.

She has a bachelor's degree in Fine Art from the University of the Arts London, a master's degree in Architecture from The Bartlett, University College London, and is a PhD candidate in Media Arts at USC School of Cinematic Arts in Los Angeles.

13.1

ALLUVIUM

Alluvium is a cinematic visualization of water flows in Death Valley.

Death Valley National Park, situated in the Mojave Desert, in the United States, is a place of extreme conditions. It has the highest temperature at 134° Fahrenheit, and the lowest altitude at -282 feet below sea level, to be recorded in North America. It is also a place with an intrinsic and unusual relationship with water. Badwater Basin, the site of this film's scenes, receives only 1.5 inches of rainfall annually, also registering it as North America's driest place. In spite of this scarcity, the landscape has a strong and tangible interrelation with water, both in the present and across millennia.

Sporadic flash floods occur in Death Valley each year, caused by heavy rainfall in the nearby Funeral Mountains. However, this is one of the few sites where rivers do not flow to the sea. Water floods through narrow canyons, incising, eroding, transporting and depositing sediment across its landscape, and with no soil or vegetation to absorb the flow, the deluge of water can move quickly and redefine the morphology of the terrain. This annual effect can be seen in soft alluvial deposits, and gravel ravines throughout the valley.

Research

The scenes in Alluvium took their starting point from the research of Dr. Noah Snyder and Lisa Kammer's research paper Dynamic adjustments in channel width in response to a forced
diversion: Gower Gulch, Death Valley National Park, California, published in the February 2008 edition of the journal Geology. Gower Gulch is a 1941 diversion of a desert wash that uncovers an expedited view of geological changes that would otherwise have taken thousands of years to unfold but have evolved at this site in several decades due to the strength of the flash floods and the conditions of the terrain.

"Our contribution focuses on changes in width in response to a dramatic change in discharge and sediment flux in a desert river, caused by a forced diversion. This anthropogenic alteration provides a rare opportunity to investigate the transient response of a system with known initial conditions, and a large signal due to a two-order-of-magnitude change in drainage area resulting in rapid rates of channel change—a situation analogous to a step-function change in climate." [1]

Gower Gulch provides a unique opportunity to see how a river responds to an extreme change in rates of water and sediment flow. At the time of the diversion, its drainage area was suddenly increased from 5 km2 to 440 km2 [2], and the team's research uncovered that the channel had consequently widened by 33 feet on average, or 66 percent [3], thus presenting effects that could mimic the impact of climate change on river flooding and discharge. The wash was originally diverted to prevent further flooding and damage to a village downstream; today it presents us with a microcosm of geological activity.

Design

Alluvium's scenes are a hybrid composition of film and digitally produced simulations. Using the technique of camera-matching, the work visualizes the phenomena of water and its geomorphological consequence, beyond human scale perception. The water flow in Gower Gulch can otherwise only be perceived through the evidence of erosion and deposition of sediment. The particle animation was developed using accurate topographic models to simulate the discharge of water over a large period. Alluvium compresses this timeframe,

providing a sense of a geological scale of time.

The work maps the velocity of the particles to their coloration, to visualize the flow and turbulence that are characteristic of fluid dynamics. The graphic technique is intended to evidence the water movement's vector, articulating the force and directionality that have aggregated the morphology of the eroded terrain. The water data has been digitally simulated, allowing the engine to produce millions of particles that both speculate on the past events of flash flooding at the site, and also envision the phenomenon that is still taking place today.

[1] Snyder, N.P., and Kammer, L.L.*, "Dynamic adjustments in channel width in response to a forced diversion: Gower Gulch, Death Valley National Park, California", Geology, 2008, v. 36, p. 187-190

[2] Schultz, L.L., "Investigation of the transient response of Gower Gulch to forced diversion, Death Valley, California" (Masters Thesis), Boston College, 2005

[3] Berdik, C., "Fast Forward: Watching The River Flow", Boston College Magazine, Spring, 2008. Accessed August 31st, 2014, http://bcm.bc.edu/issues/spring_2008/inquiring_minds/fast-forward.html

13.3

13.4

Fig. 13.3 – 13.4 The graphic technique is intended to evidence the water movement's vector, articulating the force and directionality that have aggregated the morphology of the eroded terrain.

13.5

13.6

Fig. 13.5 – 13.6 Gower Gulch is a 1941 diversion of a desert wash that uncovers an expedited view of geological changes. It provides a unique opportunity to see how a river responds to an extreme change in rates of water and sediment flow.

Fig. 13.7 – 13.8 The work maps the velocity of the particles to their coloration, to visualize the flow and turbulence that are characteristic of fluid dynamics.

13.9

13.10

Fig. 13.9 – 13.10 Alluvium's scenes are a hybrid composition of film and digitally produced simulations. Using the technique of camera-matching, the work visualizes the phenomena of water and its geomorphological consequence, beyond human scale perception.

KEIICHI MATSUDA

Keiichi Matsuda (BSc. MArch) is a designer and filmmaker. His research examines the implications of emerging technologies for human perception and the built environment. Keiichi is interested in the dissolving boundaries between virtual and physical, working with video, architecture and interactive media to propose new perspectives on the city. He has exhibited his work internationally, from London's V&A Museum to the Art Institute of Chicago, the New York MoMA, and Shanghai EXPO. He has been published extensively in print and online and has won awards for design, drawing, speaking, and filmmaking.

14.1

KEIICHI MATSUDA

Blindspot Initiative

HYPERREALITY

BY KEIICHI MATSUDA

TEXT BY JOSE SANCHEZ BASED ON INTERVIEW WITH KEIICHI MATSUDA

Matsuda's Hyperreality project is a series of design fiction videos that speculate of the future of technology. He depicts a world where augmented reality has permeated all aspects of our daily life, gamifying daily tasks and revealing information from the built environment. Matsuda's design perspective to this problem is to acknowledge the lack of organization that network providers, content makers, and the physical infrastructure will present to a highly mediatic world. He resists designing a unified experience, understanding that it would be a fallacy. The all too familiar projection of current technologies makes Matsuda's vision not as shocking as it should be, although perhaps it was once he started conceiving the project six years ago. Hyperreality forecasted the current landscape of YouTubers and bloggers, where the promiscuous generation of content has led to the rise of new internet personalities, who have become influencers for brands and companies. Matsuda envisions such a landscape operating both at a personal and urban scale.

For Matsuda, Hyperreality has become part of the brand of his practice, a design firm working at the intersection of several industries. He finds an opportunity to stay in different industries, but he also sees the value of understanding how those industries work. He reflects on how his architecture background never gave him the tools for creating his practice. 'It was never encouraged to have a business plan; you were meant to work for a design firm'. His interest and perseverance allowed him to fund his design practice which has grown to develop work for clients such as BVLGARY and Nokia.

The interest of building an audience, and allow the work to reach a larger public was always part of Matsuda's interest. Since the release of Youtube in 2005, he has been using such platforms to communicate the work and his vision. The contrast between cautionary tale and optimistic development of technology, make his films sit in a critical position, both in architecture and new media. 'I'm skeptical about technology, the way in which we learn it and consume it' explains Matsuda. He sees the public is just treated as a consumer, with no relevant role in the development of technology. His visions allow us to evaluate trends and project to a future where we can understand the consequences of products and services being developed. While he knows that companies might not like seeing the negative disruption that some of the technologies imply, by generating his critical films, Matsuda's work can establish both a critique and an optimistic re-direction for action.

Hyperreality demonstrates how the medium of architecture can be challenged to open up new conversations. The cultural and social impact of technology is not often envisioned in such a clear way as with Matsuda's work. The public interest in this piece reminds us of the public debate that architecture projects can have and perhaps must have before being implemented.

Matsuda's provocations resonate deeply with the field of architecture and design which has grown tired from the alienation of an audience and public debate. Reconnecting architectural and design thinking with both the public and with the clients, makes Matsuda's work an example living in the blindspot of current design practices.

Fig. 14.1 – 14.2 Screenshots from the hyper-reality videos displaying the social and architectural consequences of new media and augmented reality.

14.3

14.4

Fig. 14.3– 14.4 The stories are about the realities we invent for ourselves. Each short will focus on a different character and their perception of the city. Amongst the millions of overlapping fictions that make up augmented Medellin

Fig. 14.5 – 14.6 The stories will all take place over the course of a single day, woven together with many other threads of narrative that will constantly reward the observant viewer. Themes of identity, control, and delusion, will be set against a backdrop of balkanization, manipulative media channels, power struggles for data, and open-source rebellion. This is not an alien future, but rather one that is unnervingly familiar.

So tasty!
WE DELIVER
TAPAS
TAPAS
ARGOS
DHL

美好每一
EXITO
GET DOUBLE POINTS NOW!
LEVEL 99
BETTER BOD
BETTER LIF
R THE NEX
Yeastrol
Got Yeast?
Banco

3HUND

TAREK MAWAD
FRIEDERICH VAN SCHOOR

Tarek Mawad - is a German artist, specialized in 3D Art, animation and photography. His background is in projection & video art.

Since four years Tarence has been closely working with Friedrich van Schoor in an artist collective named "3hund".

Friedrich van Schoor- is a designer and media artist working in the fields of multimedia and video art.

Their collaboration "3hund" has been developed an affinity for new media projects in public space and natural environments. Their recent exhibition at Nuit Blanche and the Bioluminescent Forest project have been acclaim by the international new media arts community.

15.1

INVISIBLE TECHNOLOGY

TEXT BY JOSE SANCHEZ BASED ON INTERVIEW WITH 3HUND: FRIEDRICH VAN SCHOOR & TAREK MAWAD.

The bioluminescent forest is a projection mapping piece developed by 3hund in collaboration with Achim Treu as a composer and sound designer. The project seeks to augment our perception of nature with subtle non-narrative elements, inviting the users to project ideas into the play of lights and abstraction. By projecting a diverse range of light patterns into living entities, 3hund can construct a new hybrid reality, one that resonates with the current data culture but at the same time remains elusive from any direct reference or analogies.

3hund started this project as an opportunity to get away from day to day work and find in nature the opportunity for creative expression. The collective planned a two month film period in Palatinate forest, located close to Pirmasens in Germany. While not acknowledge being a particularly relevant location, the team found the hours of the day that were most suitable for the mood of the film. Only a 30-minute window at dawn and dusk, allowed the team to capture and recreate their vision of an augmented nature.

The project needed to convey a sense of authenticity, without explaining how the process was performed. The team intended to express the LIVE nature of the work, as the project was performed using projection mapping techniques and not post production. The journey into the forest and the DIY contraptions developed by 3hund, became an invisible infrastructure for communicating the ideas. Still, the piece can convey a sense of wonder and escape into the wild, conveying the journey and vision with its poetry.

The projection mapping techniques prove incredibly challenging within a natural environment, where wind or movement can quickly break the immersion developed by the work. The patience and perseverance of 3hund can only be understood as a new form of dialogue between their light projections and the natural medium. The proficiency to alter and create content on the spot, is a challenge often not required within a studio environment. This becomes a tool for improvisation where shots are not completely predefined but rather found in the context of their intervention.

The work of Van Schoor and Mawad seeks to augment was is already there, the bioluminescence of vegetation and animals, but taking it into an ambient communication device without a clear meaning.

The artistic freedom is one of the most celebrated assets that 3hund owns. By finding strategic timing between paid work artistic 'escapades,' they have been able to develop a brand and an identity. One that can fluidly navigate between artistic production and commercial work. The team reflects on how the technical expertise and proficiency with technology has facilitated to be opportunistic and find those 'gaps' where they enjoy full artistic freedom.

The collective continues working at the intersection of technology and nature, looking at novel ways to use new devices, and moving away from what quickly becomes trendy or over-exploited. They do not believe in recognition coming straight from using a novel device, but rather in the maturity of finding a new, unexpected angle in technologies we have available.

Their future work continues looking at new technologies such as drones, new materials or virtual and augmented reality from a different perspective, one that lives oblique to a system of expectation.

15.2

Fig. 15.1 – 15.2 The projection mapping 'bioluminescent forest'. Image shows the DIY set-up developed by 3hund for the 6-week filming schedule.

Fig. 15.3 – 15.4 The subtle beauty of a forest is illuminated with projection-mapped light in bioluminescent forest, a film by artists Friedrich van Schoor and Tarek Mawad. For six weeks, the duo immersed themselves in nature to create a "personification" of the environment, transforming trees and mushrooms into entities that glowed, sparked, and radiated with light. Set to an ethereal score by Berlin-based composer Achim Treu, the resulting film pulses with augmented life, teeming with the verdant beauty of the natural world, enhanced.

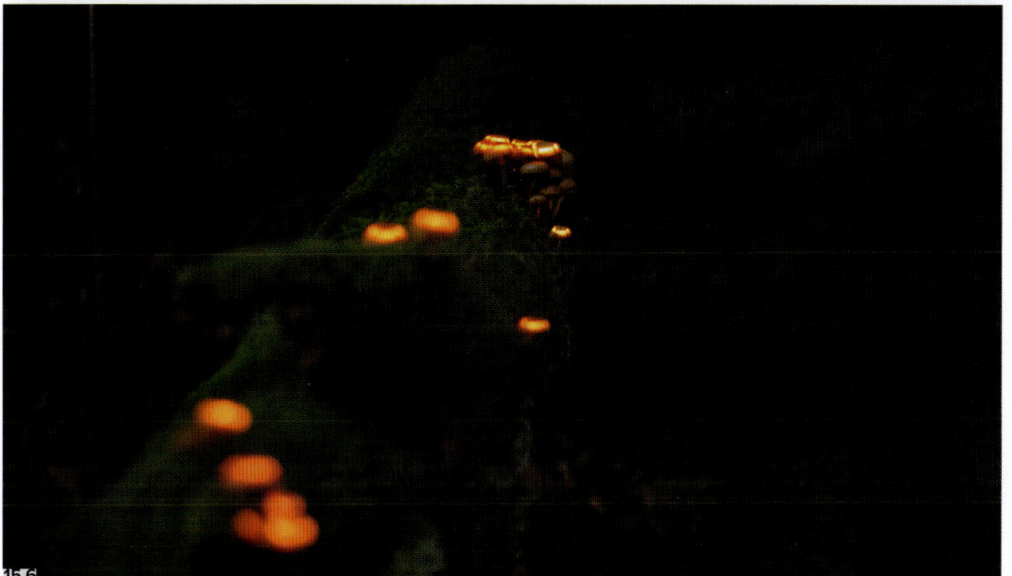

Fig. 15.5– 15.6 Hidden details of the landscape such as luminescent plants, glowing magical mushrooms, and accentuated animals were personified to highlight the natural beauty of the surroundings.

SOFTWARE

MOSTAFA ELSAYED

Mostafa ElSayed is currently working as a Senior Designer in the Computation and Design (ZHA|CODE) group at Zaha Hadid Architects, London, where his responsibilities currently include developing design research and maintaining computational platforms.

He is also a course tutor in the Design Research Lab (DRL) at the Architectural Association School of Architecture, and his work has been published in various publication including SIMAUD 2011/2014 proceedings and ICFF 2012, amongst others.

As is a graduate of the AA and the American University of Sharja, Mostafa has taught and presented work at various events, workshops and institutions both in London and internationally including the AA, UCL, RCA, University of Applied Arts Vienna, AUS, TEC de Monterrey, SCI-ARC.

So what button do I press again? A question that is becoming increasingly the default inquiry by students pursuing a degree in architecture or other design majors and I suspect a question that is oft repeated in offices as well. However this article focus does not revolve around the proliferation of digital design software or the merits of using those tools, this article will focus however on the recent rise in designers focusing on the computational processes and methods they employ almost as much as if not more than the focus they place on the end- product these processes produce.

Eventually, designers who choose to engage algorithms and their primarily code-based workflows as design tools start to become interested in the process of making these tools more intuitive and accessible to the wider design community. This is where things get interesting as we now have a group of designers who have graduated from successfully exploiting the potentials of algorithmic design to the process of packaging their gained intuition and custom workflows into software solutions for their fellow designers. The following chapter showcases some examples of this idea and shows how the main advantage arising from designers creating software around their design workflows is the democratization of their knowledge and intuitions. This is a process that will have to become more commonplace if we are to demystify our methods as a progressive design community and allowing others to engage our work on the design level. Defining and designing that engagement, is in my opinion, the only way we will remain critical and relevant in a time where increasingly complex problems are simplified into apps and 'one click' interfaces.

So first off, what kind of processes are we talking about here? That is something that needs to be defined before we can move on to discussing how to allow others to engage in these processes. A common thread in the examples played out in this chapter is that they are primarily processes and workflows that depend on controlling and biasing algorithmically driven systems through control parameters and logic. Also, these systems are usually goal driven and more often than not these goals are not explicitly relatable to the desired outcome by the user, by which I mean the goal of a cellular automata system is not to design an interesting pattern but rather to play out the growth described in its simple rule logic. This dichotomy brings us to the crucial role of a designer working with these systems, that of the curator. This role involves the designer being firstly an observant of the system playing out its logic and secondly a careful curator of its parameters, learning to calibrate them to achieve desired effects and outcomes.

Ultimately, this process contributes to a designers intuition regarding the control of the process and its outcomes, and it is this intuition that acts as the main barrier to entry for others looking to employ these methods in their design workflow. Therefore, when designing how we communicate with the systems, a designer is usually concerned with converting this intuition into the experience that will dictate the usability and eventually the usefulness of the software. In my experience, there are two ways of carrying out this conversion, the more established problems of user interaction or interface and the less common but increasingly important presence of assistive heuristics or 'learning' present in the software's logic.

As the processes and methods, we use as designers increase in their complexity, it is becoming more important to utilize methods that assist and simplify the process, both in passive and active fashions. It is through these actions that the designer of the software should look to employ the burgeoning field of machine learning. However, unlike other domains were this term is burdened with conversations regarding the efficacy and ethics of artificial intelligence, luckily the creative domains fall under a set of problems that are considered AI complete or AI hard, meaning that solving these problems is akin to solving the main artificial intelligence problem of making computers as intelligent as humans. Therefore, machine learning fits more of an augmented intelligence model, meaning that while an intelligently augmented software does play a more participatory and active role in the design processes, this participation is manifest primarily as an augmentation to the end users intelligence. Acting to guide the user through the workflow or suggesting modifications to their current inputs or even running the entire process and simply seeking the user's approval at key stages of its workflow.

Ironically, the most prevalent form of heuristic augmentation in design involves this computational intelligence outsourcing some of its decisions out to you, the human agent, to further its problem-solving. This is especially clear when it comes to exploring the increasingly large and multi-dimensional solutions spaces we are increasingly trying to navigate as designers. This has been a problem monopolized by algorithms such as genetic algorithms and other 'search' methods. However, this is not the category of algorithms that can benefit designers the most as they are slow and prone to calibration errors.

Conversely, the heuristic methods that would aid or augment the design process the most would be those that work to present the complex in simple terms, those that reduce a set of solutions or results into their common patterns and properties. By looking at complex processes or simulations or workflows through a lens of abstraction, we can easily find commonalities and make assumptions regarding them. Therefore, leading to us being to present those assumptions and commonalities to the end user and allowing them to work off of those assumptions and exploit the new found understanding of the system.

To put this in context, we can use processes a lot of designers are increasingly familiar with, which is that of simulation. The process of playing out a set of parameter defined rules across time to an eventual state of convergence. Usually, this process is time-consuming and more importantly, incredibly sensitive to initial conditions and rule sets.

If we take an example of particles being integrated into a vector field, a simulation a lot of us are familiar with perhaps more regarding its output, streamlines. We can see that the simulation is quite time intensive and it is quite hard to understand the role of any one parameter in the system such as the strength of the vector field or the mass of the particles or even harder the shape of the field. However, if we abstract the simulation space into its constituent components and graph those components out, it becomes easy to see trends and patterns in the data, and if these trends are apparent to us, they can be taught to a machine. This is where the 'learning' part comes in, using simple algorithms that fall under the category of 'supervised learning', which basically means that we are aware of the pattern or ground truth in the data we can teach the machine to see them as well. This is done through primarily optimisation and data transformation techniques such as linear regression and Principal Component Analysis. By using these methods, we cut down on simulation times since now that the computer has learned the patterns present in the simulation space it can make reasonable predictions as to its outcome. Ultimately though the main benefit of the computer 'learning' space is that it can know act as an augmenting agent in the user's experience of working with the simulation as a design tool. Since it can suggest meaningful edits and bias user input to more successful or fruitful areas of the simulation space, actively acting as a participant in a collaborative workflow.

Ironically, a majority of designers would believe that the process of opening up and simplifying the processes that we work with day in and day out, would somehow cheapen our professions and usually these conversations end up with the edict that this way of thinking would only serve to replace or reduce the importance of the trained designer. However, there is a lot to be appreciated regarding our workflows by trying to make them accessible through others, and the more we aim to abstract predict and structure the information we produce the more the professionals and their end users will benefit.

PANAGIOTIS MICHELATOS & ANDREW PAYNE

Panagiotis Michalatos is an architect and assistant professor in architecture at the Harvard Graduate School of Design. Between 2006 and 2010 he worked as a computational design researcher for the London based structural engineering firm AKT. While in AKT along with colleague Sawako Kaijima they provided consultancy and designed computational solutions for a range of high profile projects. They have also developed a range of software applications for the intuitive and creative use of structural engineering methods in design. Panagioti's work in interaction design and digital media has resulted in a long-lasting collaboration with Stockholm based contemporary dance company CCAP.

Andrew Payne is an architect and Senior Building Information Specialist at CASE. He holds a Doctoral degree from Harvard's Graduate School of Design where his research focused on personalized intelligent comfort control strategies for office buildings. Andrew's other research interests include embedded computation, parametric design, robotics, programmable microcontrollers, and 3d printing. He is the co-author and lead developer of Firefly – a software plugin which bridges the gap between the digital CAD environment of Rhino/Grasshopper with physical input/output devices like the Arduino, webcams, mobile phones, game controllers and more.

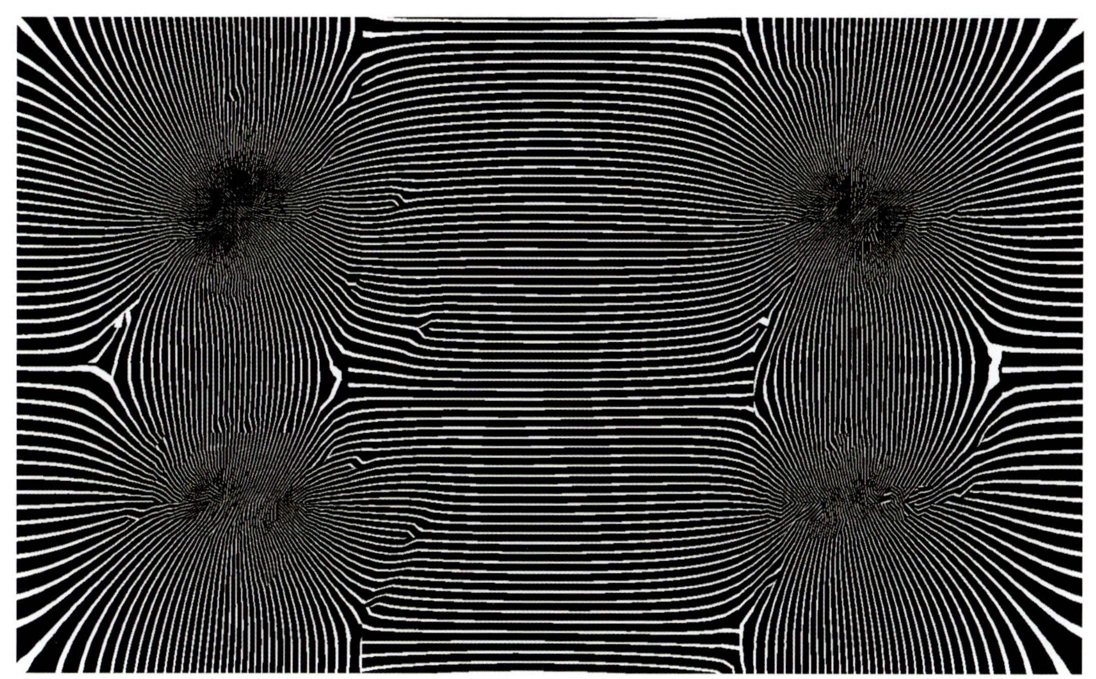

MONOLITH

In 2D graphics, there are two prevailing paradigms that are used to represent geometry. Vector graphics - which use mathematical expressions to represent shapes or polygons on a computer screen – are lightweight, efficient, and scalable. They often perform poorly at blending or compositing shapes together. Raster graphics, on the other hand, use a dense array of pixels, each of which contains information stored in channels (i.e., Red, Green, and Blue), to draw objects on a monitor, paper, or some other medium. In general vector graphics have a higher degree of accuracy and a smaller memory footprint. However, they are inadequate in representing dense spatial variations and performing certain types of blending and filtering operations that are characterized by topological changes.

If we were to extend these two paradigms into the third dimension, we would find that the distribution of CAD tools is largely biased toward a vector-like representation. One that describes objects simply as a patchwork of surfaces which form a boundary between solid and void. This type of modeling technique is known as a boundary representation, or 'B-rep' for short. While efficient, B-reps often suffer from many of the same pitfalls found in its 2D counterpart.

In B-reps, material representations are often treated as homogeneous and discontinuous. With existing design tools, a designer has no way to manipulate or visualize the distribution of material in the interior of an object. In many cases, this limitation was not noticeable primarily because current fabrication techniques could not manipulate materials at this level of detail and therefore there was little need for such representations outside complex finite element models. Most design software used by architects has its origins in mechanical engineering and often implies an assembly paradigm inherited from the industrial revolution. However 3D visualization and modeling techniques are increasingly influenced by developments in the biomedical field, which because of its subject matter is concerned with distributions of matter more than assemblies of discrete components.

As digital fabrication techniques such as multi-material 3D printing have enabled greater precision and control over the deposition and mixing of materials, the digital tools that we use to model and visualize design artifacts have simply proven inadequate. To overcome these barriers, we set out to design a new type of volumetric modeling environment, called Monolith, which is capable of treating space as a continuum of variable densities and material properties. We know that objects found in nature are capable of complex structures where the variability of material is defined at a multiplicity of scales and according to various functional criteria. To create models with material distributions which vary throughout its volume, we needed to rethink the fundamental data structure that we were working with.

We think that voxels present a better alternative to traditional surface modeling techniques. What's a voxel? Well, think of it as a three-dimensional pixel. In fact, the word voxel is short for volumetric pixel. Much like a pixel, which describes the attributes (like color) of an element within a larger composition (an image); a voxel can describe the attributes of a physical location within a 3D volume. These attributes can include information about its material properties, density, color, and more.

The benefits of using a voxel representation include the ability to perform operations typically only reserved for 2D image editing and analysis applications. Filtering,

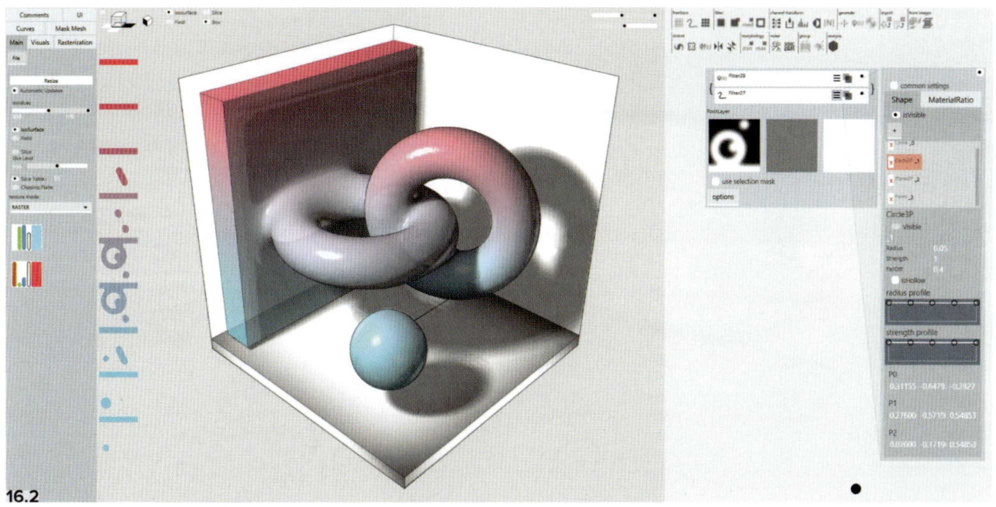

Fig. 16.1 Creation of anisotropic elastic material. By manipulating the orientation of the grain of the mixing between the two materials [soft and hard] we can control how an object responds to bending.

Fig. 16.2 Monolith user interface

such as blurring/softening, histogram equalization, and convolution, for example, can be applied in three dimensions using a voxel-based representation, with little modification. Monolith also can employ 2D techniques such as painting and localized interactive editing (i.e., blurring, smearing, twisting, etc.), but extends them to three dimensions because of the underlying voxel representation.

Using a raster-based representation, such as a voxel, also gives the designer the ability to control microscopic patterns of structure within the 3D volume. Micro patterns can be generated using 2D images, 3D voxel patterns, or procedural textures. The visual appearance of the model after applying these patterns can be rendered in real time using a custom volumetric shader. Alternatively, the volumetric information can be translated into a series of bitmaps, each corresponding to a layer within the 3D printed volume, which can be used to print patterns that would be difficult if not impossible using existing techniques. For example, printing structural artificial grain or optical lenses with customized micro-patterning would be impractical if each part of the geometry had to be exported as a series of triangulated meshes.

And while raster-based techniques offer a lot of opportunities, that doesn't mean we should discount the benefits of CAD modeling. There is, after all, a reason why surface modeling (i.e., B-rep) has become the dominant 3D modeling paradigm among designers and architects. Much like vector graphics; surface modeling is computationally efficient, scalable, and parameterized. This makes for a straightforward and agile modeling process.

Monolith can generate voxelized data from source geometry such as points, lines, curves, planes, and BREPs. The process involves measuring the distance from each voxel to the nearest point on the

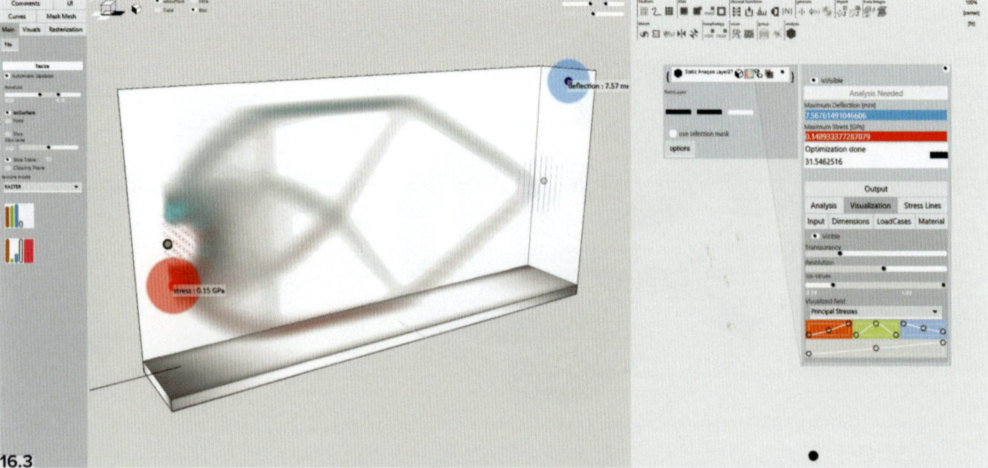

16.3

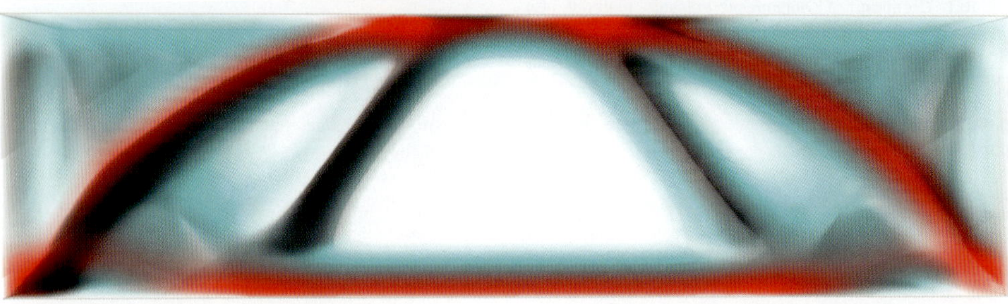

16.4

Fig. 16.3 User interface for structural analysis and optimization within monolith

Fig. 16.4 Topologically optimal distribution of high strength material within softer matrix resulting in a beam/truss hybrid. As there is no sharp boundary between soft and hard material, certain stress concentration effects are avoided.

Fig. 16.5 Three dimensional stress lines. Using monolith's structural analysis module, which can generate the full three-dimensional stress line pattern within a volume of material, in combination with the ability to 3d print curves directly without the need of fine meshes, we can visualize the stress patterns within a complex shape. This is also a demonstration of the possibility of 3d print fine reinforcement patterns with future 3d printers.

Fig. 16.6 Anisotropic transparency. Using monolith's 3d typographic capabilities, a variable micropattern is generated throughout the geometry. As sides of the micropattern align and misalign depending on viewing angle the transparency and light penetration through the material is modulated.

Fig. 16.7 Topologically optimal cantilevering slab reinforcement. The emergent leaf-like structure of hard material within the softer transparent material is reminiscent of venation patterns found in nature.

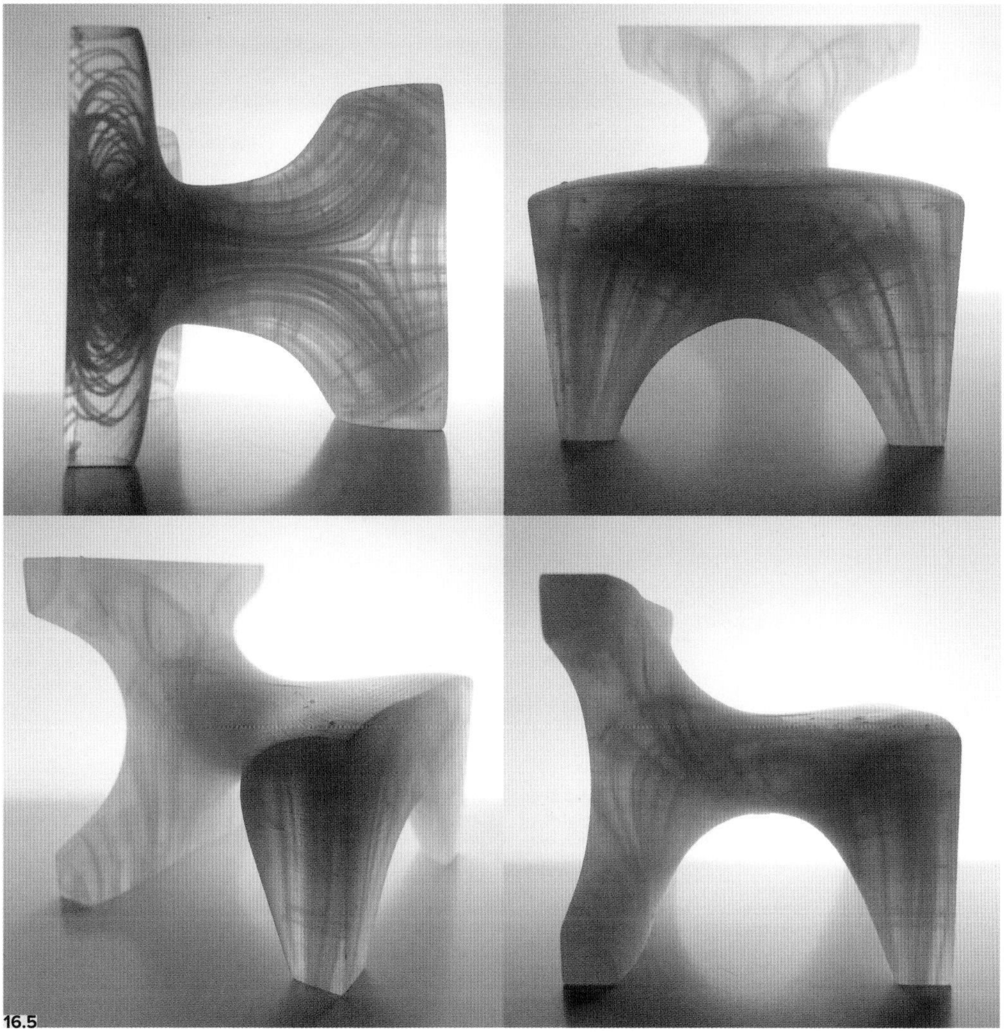

16.5

16.6

16.7

Fig. 16.8 Grid-based voxel editing with different interpolation functions. The user can easily set the individual weights of grid points whose influence/ density gets interpolated with their neighbors to achieve various shape qualities.

Fig. 16.9 Application of Gaussian blurring on a medical data set imported from a series of tomographic slices.

Fig. 16.10 Boolean operations with voxelized models can be smooth since the Boolean operands can be fuzzy fields rather than solids with sharp boundaries

Fig. 16.11 Voxelization of the Stanford bunny in monolith and subsequent application of a Gaussian blur. This enables the mixing of conventional mesh-based modeling with voxel-based techniques.

source geometry. After passing through a scalar decay function (i.e., linear, square, exponential, or power), these distances are normalized and assigned to the corresponding shape or material ratio channel. Mesh geometry can also be used to inform voxel densities.

Because Monolith takes advantage of techniques found in both traditional CAD design tools and image editing and analysis applications (only extended to three dimensions), we refer to it as a "hybrid" modeling environment. With the techniques outlined in Monolith, designers have an unprecedented degree of control spanning scales from the micro to the macro. Digital design environments have been criticized for being scale-less often misleading designers to apply identical modeling techniques to radically different objects (from a coffee cup to a city). We propose not a scale-less design but a multi-scale design approach where one can traverse and define properties of materiality across multiple scales.

Fig. 16.12 Fine stress line pattern within a slab. In this sample, we used monolith to print out dense bundles of hairlines [each curve has the minimum allowed thickness by the printer being one resin dot thick].

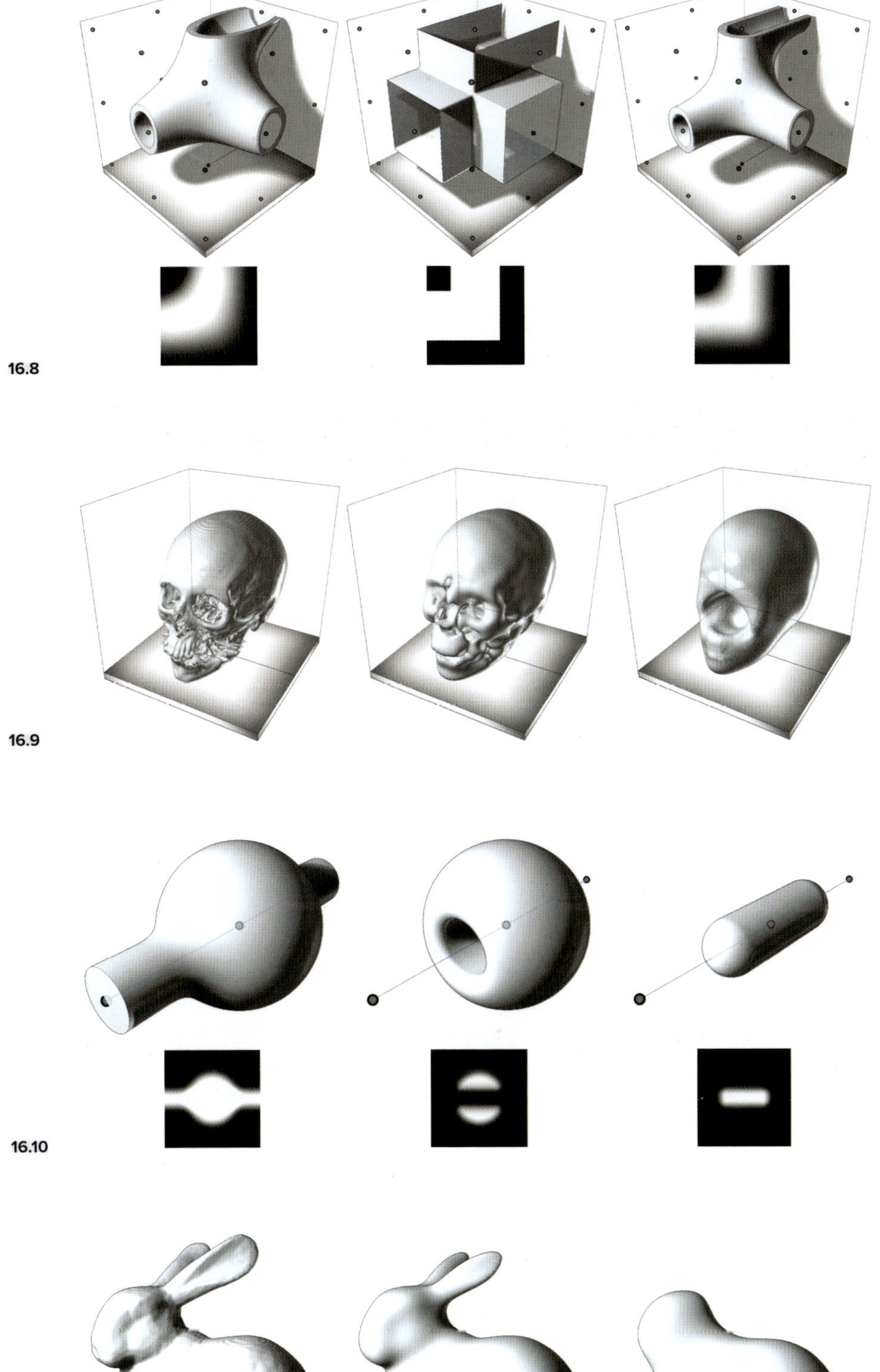

16.8

16.9

16.10

16.11

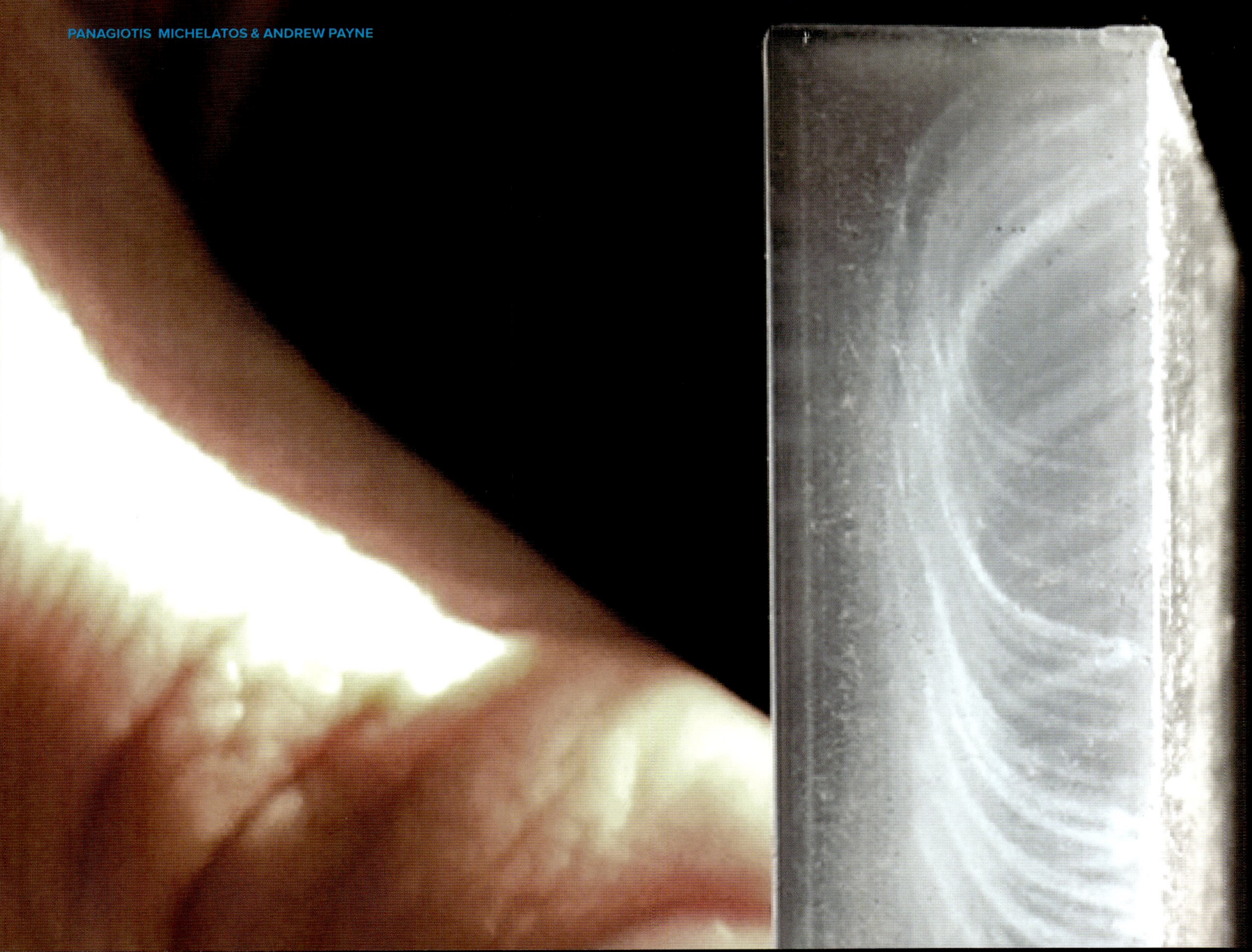

M. CASEY REHM

M. Casey Rehm is a designer and algorithmic consultant based in Los Angeles. He received a MSAAD from Columbia University in 2009 and his BARCH from Carnegie Mellon University in 2005. He has over ten years of architectural experience, working for firms in New York, Los Angeles, Berlin, and London. In addition to his professional experience, Casey has been a full-time faculty member at Rensselaer Polytechnic Institute, assisted studios at Columbia University, the University of Pennsylvania, and the Pratt Institute and taught workshops at The University of Kentucky. Currently, he teaches graduate design studios and seminars in programming and robotics in design at SCI-Arc in Los Angeles.

17.1

COMPOSITION THROUGH INHUMAN PERCEPTION

The exploration of design techniques using extensive algorithms (engaging information external to the program) has been a central theme to work done by Kinch. As a civilization the techniques for measuring and accumulating information have reached a level of intensity, that the ability of traditional methods for intelligently engaging this data has become ineffectual. Many disciplines outside of architecture have begun to embrace the use intelligent agent-based algorithms as a method extracting value and produce effective interactions from this glut of data. These methods have become so prevalent that there are few aspects of our daily life which are not mediated by these applications, which has produced transformations to our culture and human behavior. As architects designing for this transforming culture, we need to understand the systems which drive and interject our disciplinary intentions into them at the level of intensity relevant to these mediators. The discourse around architecture should shift towards interface as opposed to shape or form and our design of spaces driven not by reductive diagrams, but the needs (or lack of specific need) of the granular users.

If our design algorithms are to engage external data and benefit from its embodied intelligence, it is important to also investigate the modes of perception available to our systems. The quantity of libraries, papers and open source software surrounding machine vision in relationship to image and video and the relative clarity to their function suits their use as a basis for exploring new forms of design. The abundance of these resources reflects areas of cultural reality, whether it's the necessity to find intelligence in massive quantities of surveillance video or in our desire to portray highly curated image driven narratives of ourselves across social media (if those are two separate things). Additionally, the fact that these algorithms specifically deal with issues of image and representation makes them seductive territory for the architectural designer as a basis for exploring the design of agent behaviors. The two-dimensional nature of these applications and the constraint of the pixel-based media they inhabit further aids in the perception of cause and effect when programming design intelligence.

The design of the Striated Vistas[1] installations, a series of collaborations with photographer Yuna Yagi, requires a design approach which differs from those of static images and film. Kinch's brief was to produce a system which runs for an indeterminate amount of time (weeks) and intelligently engage previously unknown media as it's content. In this case, the photographer, Yuna Yagi, continuously uploaded her photographic work into the machine over the course of the exhibition and the machine seamlessly manipulates it into a coherent composition. The designer then must produce a machine which can autonomously and endlessly evaluate and manipulate the screen, never repeating but always generating coherent yet differentiated imagery. Traditional techniques of composition, representation, and curation have dubious relevance. The machine inherently tends to one of two extremes. On the one hand, over the course of several weeks, the machine could tend towards entropic degradation resulting in a reduction of intelligent heterogeny. On the other hand, totalistic techniques of image preservation could push the piece into territories of anachronistic collage, engaging the viewer exclusively through dated tropes of repetition, juxtaposition, alignment, translation etc...

To produce a durable balance between these extremes the machine utilizes two simultaneous intelligent agencies operating in opposition. One set of agents operates at the level of the single

Fig.17.2 Still from Striated Vistas 1.0 with Yuna Yagi's photographs as inputs

pixel. Their behavior is divorced from anthropocentric tendencies and develops emergent patterning exclusively through an awareness of their color value and that of their neighboring pixels. The agents explore color relationships within the image translating color values throughout the field through a form of competition. While the resultant effects appear intricate, it represent a reduction of heterogeneity, as stronger color sets (per their game) replace the subtly varying hues of the original imagery. In this way, the agents act to reduce the embodied color information of the photographs while exposing underlying color structures.

The other set of agents operates through more anthropocentric collaging methods., and are referred to as healers within the vernacular of the studio. These healers introduce unadulterated image content from the uploaded photographs though multiple scales of pixel regions in a generational cycle of birth and death. The graphic content of this behavior relies on human perception through the photographer to define the intelligence of the pixel relationships, unlike the other's purely color based ordering principles. While on the surface this system seems to exist in a territory of more traditional collage techniques, and in fact, the orthogonally constrained propagation of the system is meant to introduce elements of a totalistic aesthetic into the overall system, it's behaviors are also rooted in machine vision algorithms. Several methods have been used over the course of the series to drive the position and

17.3

17.4

Fig. 17.3 – 17.4 Two views of a three-dimensional implementation of the color based behaviors used in the Striated Vistas projects. These are images a portion of a speculative project on libraries. In this case, the voxels sample initial color values from three axes and then initiate a three dimensional version of the pixel behaviors developed in 2D.

Fig. 17.5 Two stills from a real-time implementation of the pixel behaviors utilized in the Striated Vistas series to produce augmented interactive mirrors. The first image composites and records its reflection over time. The bottom image superimposes local reflections from the Kinch office space with streaming video from a highway overpass near Kyoto.

17.5

Fig.17.6 Interior Perspective, New Market for Instanbul
Competition entry by Kinch

translation of the healer agents. In the first generations of the machine, the initial positions are determined independently from the image content they carry but are generated by searching for regions in the current frame where the other set of agents has been allowed to operate past a preset level of degradation (Fig. 17.2, and cover). This version of the behavior is developed to be antagonistic to the other set of agents and operates to balance the composition over time. Later versions of the healers generate their initial positions and behaviors based on the graphic content of the image they are introducing into the composition (Fig. 17.7 and Fig. 17.8). Various blob detection, contrast analysis, and shape finding algorithms are used to determine the most figurally intensive or graphically interesting regions of the new photograph and locate the healers [2]. The first strategy works to create balance through an even distribution of disruptive agent and healer populations; the second achieves balance by continuously introducing the maximum amount of heterogeneity with the healers to the canvas to counteract the reductive quality of the other agents.

The result of these two adversarial agencies is a composition which can fluctuate towards intensities of both stochastic and ordered aesthetics without ever residing for too long in either. Over the course of several weeks, the composition will endlessly change, never repeat, yet still, maintain a coherent aesthetic position while exposing relationships between

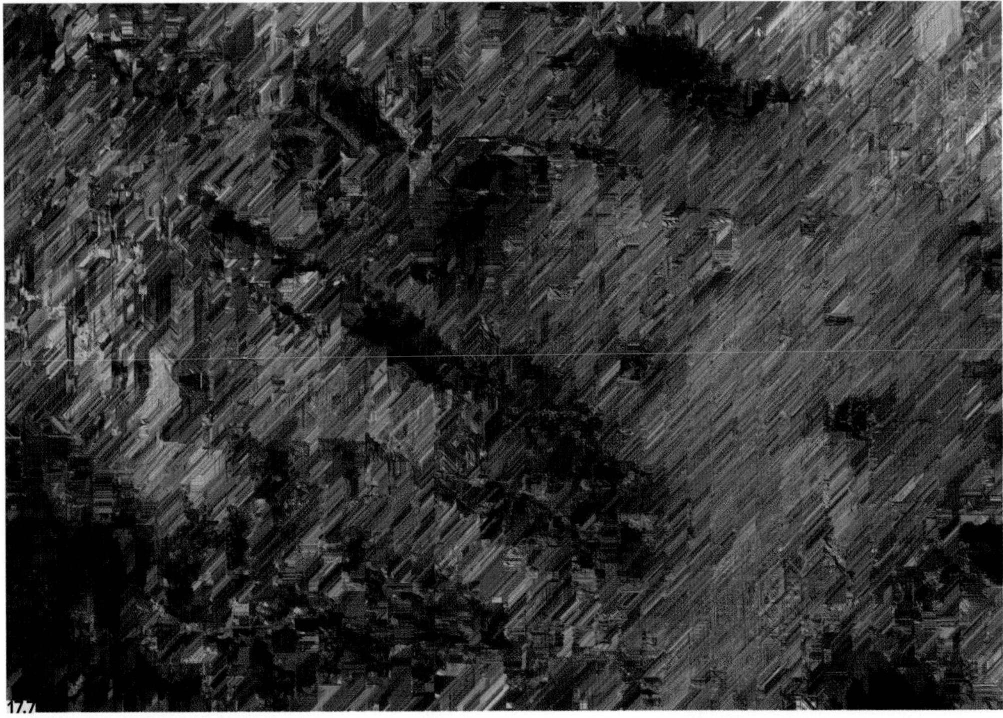

Fig.17.7 Tree finding variation on BlindSpot cover series.

Fig.17.8 Still from Straited Vistas 2.0 app with floral still lifes as inputs.

photographs. The specific discoveries made from this project have begun to permeate the other work in the studio, as levels of interactivity, the breadth of sensing devices, and spatiality of the work increases. Whether it's ordering drone captured photographs into large-scale drawings, generating spatial organization and materiality (Fig. 17.7), or producing ambient interactive digital mirrors, the significance of a systems methods of perceptions on their design output are inextricable.

[1] Striated Vistas V1.0, "It's a One World" Gallery 23, Kyoto 2015 with Yuna Yagi
Striated Vistas V2.0, "KG+" Gallery ABC, Kyoto 2015 with Yuna Yagi
The application was developed in Processing 2.2.1
Reas, Casey, and Ben Fry. Processing. 2013. Retrieved from https://processing.org/

[2] The following libraries were used in Processing:
Borenstein, Greg (2015) OpenCV for Processing.
Retrieved from https://github.com/atduskgreg/opencv-processing
Gachadoat, Julien (2012) BlobDetection.
Retrieved from http://www.v3ga.net/processing/BlobDetection/

Blindspot Initiative

PLETHORA-PROJECT

JOSE SANCHEZ

Jose Sanchez is an Architect / Game Developer based in Los Angeles, California. He is partner at Bloom Games, start-up built upon the BLOOM project, winner of the WONDER SERIES hosted by the City of London for the London 2012 Olympics. He is the director of the Plethora Project, a research and learning project investing in the future of online open-source knowledge. He is also the creator of Block'hood, a city simulator video game exploring notions of crowd-sourced urbanism named by the Guardian one of the most anticipated games of 2016.

He has taught and guest lectured in several renowned institutions across the world, including the Architectural Association in London, the University of Applied Arts in Vienna, ETH Zurich, The Bartlett School of Architecture, University College London.

Today, he is an Assistant Professor at USC School of Architecture in Los Angeles. His research 'Gamescapes', explores generative interfaces in the form of video games, speculating in modes of intelligence augmentation, combinatorics, and open systems as a design medium.

18.1

BLOCK'HOOD
SYSTEMS THINKING GAMES

Block'hood is a video game developed by Jose Sanchez, director of the Plethora Project and assistant professor at the University of Southern California.
The video game is a vertical city simulator that focuses on ideas of ecology and entropy inviting players to design and simulate the systemic relationships of neighborhoods.

Block'hood was initially inspired by the Whole Earth Catalog, a publication from the 60's that would document technologies and DIY solutions for farming and living. Architects like Buckminster Fuller were great supporters of this initiative. The catalog would only be an index of objects and techniques to be further explored by the readers.
By rethinking the catalog as a video-game where each one of this technologies or possibilities, could be simulated and combined with one another, a new layer of participation and value could be generated; one in which the imagination and gameplay of a participant could foster local innovation.

Block'hood situates itself as a game that can breach the digital and physical space by modeling data allowing a player to learn and speculate how the use of resources could be managed systemically. Inspired by an urban farming facility in Chicago, Block'hood core mechanic is that of eliminating waste. Each unit in the game is a productive entity that can produce new resources once requirements are met. The requirements are the inputs that each unit need to become productive. In this way, the inputs and outputs of all units create a system of interdependence, where everything is linked to everything else. This is the first ecological concept presented by the game, and a player soon discovers the necessity in considering this environmental implication to progress.
Block'hood also presents ideas of entropy by simulating the decay of each block as time passes. A unit without enough inputs will increase its decay level to the point in which it will break or become abandoned. This is based on each unit's resilience level. In practical terms, players will see their buildings collapse if they don't consider the ecological interdependencies of the units.

At any point, a player can switch and see the data driving the system. The player can decide to see key variables such as decay, accessibility of units, the productivity of units or structural integrity. By visualizing the data driving the process, the player can slowly learn new architectural concepts and see how to generate patterns that optimize the use of resources. By not hiding anything to the player, the game expects to develop expertise and mastery, allowing the human intuition of a player to be coupled with the rigorous algorithmic intelligence of the system. Seeking what J.C.R. Licklider called Man-computer symbiosis.

These simple rules allow for a game that is easy to learn but very difficult to master. The open-ended nature of the system provides that players can be creative and explore the infinite amount of permutations, discover solutions and designs that are completely unexpected, even to the developer team.

The game was designed in a modular and scalable manner, allowing the growth of the system over time. Instead of simulating a city as a centralized idea, the game focuses on the discreteness of the units, and the operations that each unit can have over one another. In this sense Block'hood could be extrapolated to a deck of cards, where the information of each discrete unit could allow many 'games' or rulesets to be played. This would allow for the software to become a research engine for urban design; allowing players to speculate on

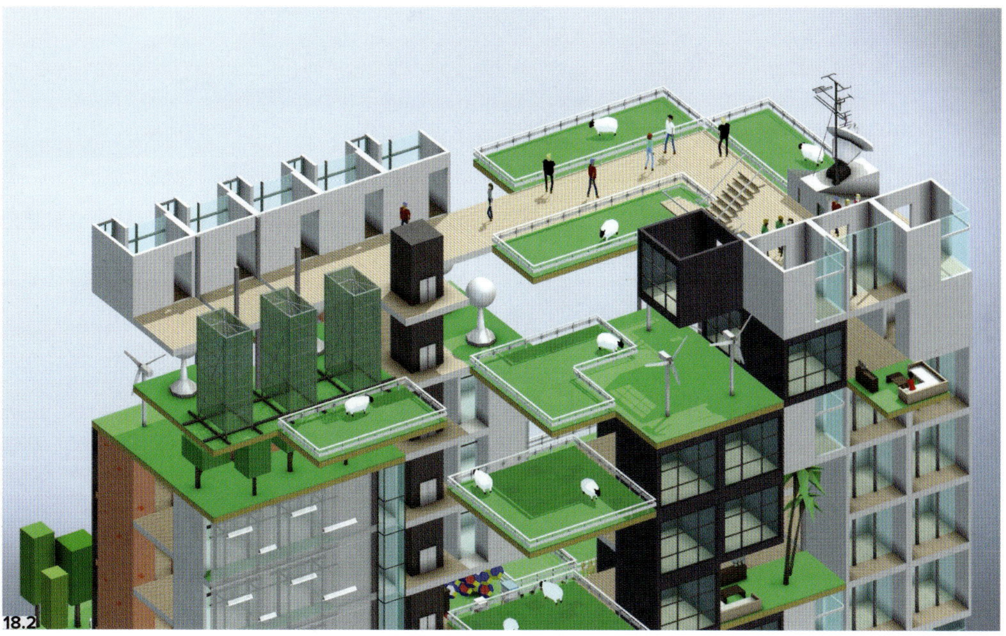
18.2

the value of units, the impact of the design of new units or speculative currencies that might affect the dependencies and hierarchies that emerge from interactions.

The main purpose of deciding to do a video game and not a design software deals with the critical metric of public engagement, attempting to reach a much larger audience than a specialized design community. By having a much larger player pool, the engine can generate more divergent results that could live in the blind spot of trained designers.

Block'hood situates itself as a game for education and creativity where the creations of players could both educate but also contribute to the development of patterns for ecological cities. A project that deals with the ethics of crowdsourcing not by creating a competitive platform to harvest the labor of players, but rather a collaborative open source environment, where sharing of designs and recipes is encouraged. The value of players creations is in the hands of players and the community, not in the hands of the author of the system.

The game was released in May 2017 and to the time of this writing, counts with a community of over 90.000 users.

Acknowledgments:

Game has been created and developed by Jose Sanchez of Plethora-Project, with the design support of Bryan Zhang, Gentaro Makinoda, Alan Hung, Jingbo Yan, Kellan Cartledge, Petr Yakyamsev, and the music of Selma Mutal.

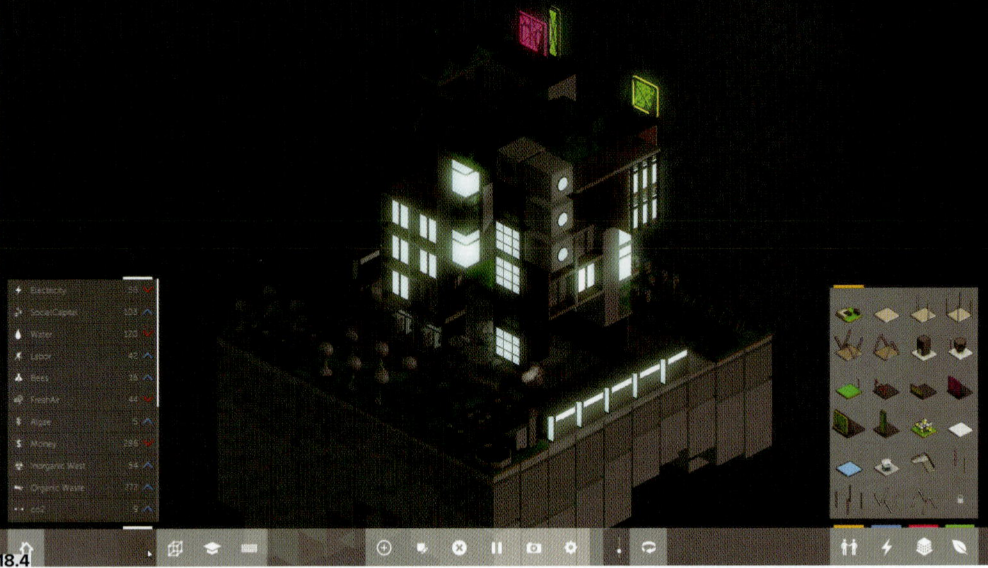

Fig. 18.3 – 18.4 Each Block you create has Inputs and Outputs. For Example, a tree might need water to create oxygen, and a shop might need consumers to create money. By understanding how each block is dependent on other blocks, you can create a productive network. Make sure to optimize your production and generate abundant resources. The game has 20+ resources that are specific to every block, so the number of relations are enormous!

18.5

Fig. 18.5 If Blocks don't get the inputs they need, they will decay over time. Slowly becoming abandoned or being destroyed. Once a Block is abandoned or destroyed, you will have to remove it and avoid it from making other blocks decay further. Be careful... seeking a utopian neighborhood carelessly, can lead to dystopia.

JOSE SANCHEZ

MANUEL JIMENEZ

Manuel Jimenez Garcia, a registered architect in the UK and Spain, with a background in computer programming and interactive design, is the founder and director of MadMDesign, a London based research practice, which mainly focuses on the integration of computational processes and digital fabrication. Manuel is currently developing an open source Java application called Soft-modelling, the resulting prototypes of this software have been exhibited at the London Clerkenwell Design Week 2013-14, Resonate 2014 (Belgrade) and Acadia 2014 Design Agency (Los Angeles).

His previous projects on catenary structures and digital materialism were featured in at Royal Academy Summer Exhibition (London) and Acadia 2012 Synthetic Digital Ecologies (San Francisco).

Alongside his practice, Manuel is currently Course Master of AD Research Cluster 4, as well as Unit Master of MArch Unit 19, both at The Bartlett School of Architecture (UCL)(London); he is also co-curator of the Bartlett Computational Plexus and Programme Director at the Architectural Association's Visiting School in Madrid (AAVSM). He has taught and run workshops at Architectural Association's Design Research Laboratory (AADRL) (London), Polytechnic University of Architecture (Madrid), European University Madrid and L'École Spéciale d'Architecture (Paris).

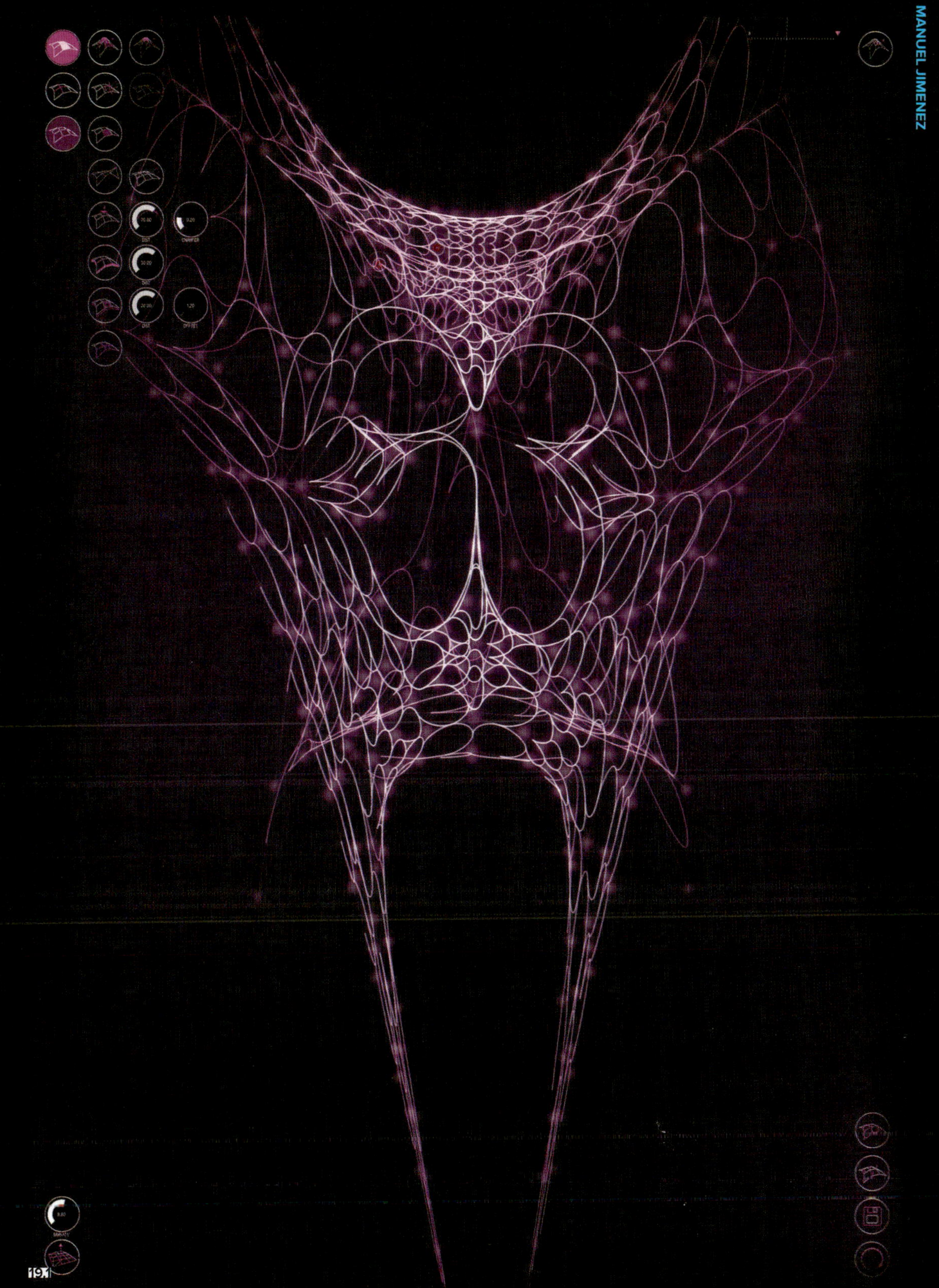

19.1

SOFTMODELING

Contemporary advanced simulation software allows, on the one hand, a more accurate understanding of material behavior at an architectural scale, and one the other, as a form-finding methodology. The potential of continual structural evaluation in form-finding allows for the morphology of an architectural system to be informed by physical laws instead of mathematical definitions in real-time, enabling the evaluation of multiple iterations of the same system to happen simultaneously.

However, despite the increasing tendency to utilize these software in architectural design research methodologies as a means of solving multiple variations of a (structural, material) system, there has not been many attempts to rethink the more generic digital tools that architects utilize today. This is an opportunity to begin to question and interrogate the way we utilise these tools, with a particular interest in how to incorporate open-source tools into or against the more generic software that are now increasingly used daily by architects. Thus far, the development of open source tools has remained largely within the problem-solving linked to specific architectural projects or problems. SoftModelling on the other hand, is an open source Java application developed to address not only a specific project but also can cover the basic function of digital design software. Its code is open source and easy to manipulate to facilitate the creation of multiple versions suitable for different users.

Most kinds of modeling software recompute the order of edges when any mesh operation is given. This is why a two-step process is normally utilized since the serial numbers of the particle-springs will not match the new edges' serial numbers after this operation occurs. Soft modeling develops a strategy for each of the mesh operations to solve this. First, the app relocates the serial numbers of each edge on the mesh to maintain parity between the particle-springs linked to them. Then, instead of a recompilation of the particle-spring system, a detailed analysis of the mesh identifies the parts that have been modified, without affecting the rest of the object. This process not only improves the efficiency of the physics simulation but facilitates a seamless integration between modeling and simulation. The synchronization of particles – vertices/ springs to edges – enables the constant updating of the positions of each part of the model. What one model is automatically physics, and vice versa. There is constant feedback between the physical behavior of every particle-spring of the 3D mesh subdivision as well as the variable scale and depth at every point, which leads to an output that is both physically and geometrically precise. This improves flexibility for the designer as one can modify and simulate simultaneously within a single software, as well as edit the GUI and the source code. It establishes an understanding that particle-spring systems cannot only be used as a global framework, but as a step-by-step transformative process for architectural design.

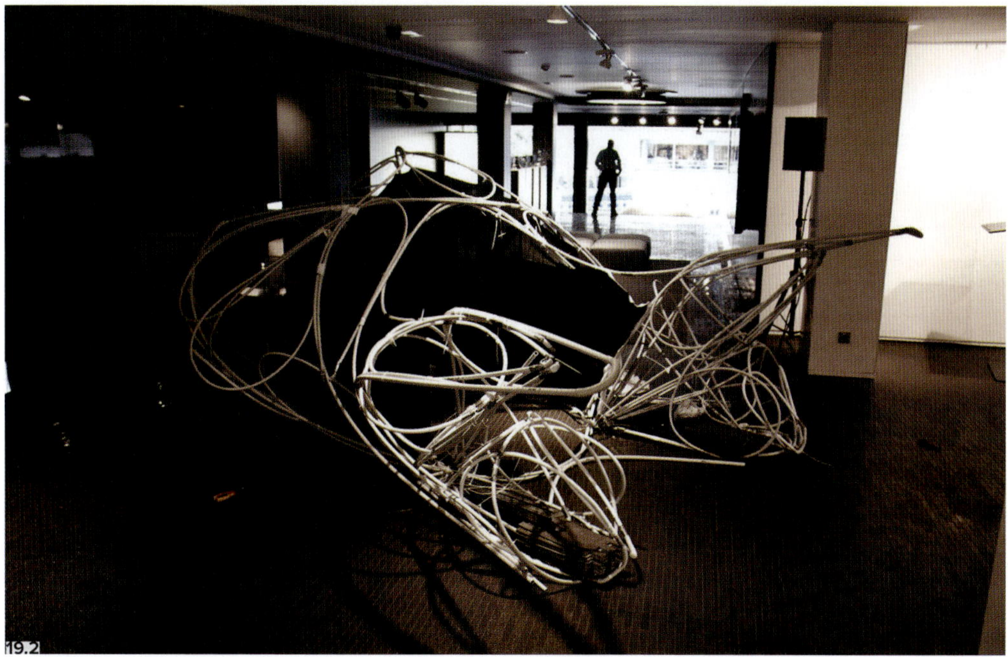

19.2

Fig. 19.1 Soft modelling 3.0. - Simulation software interface developed for Processing. Render mode with active conversion from faces to linear elements. The multiple bent elements connect to create a structure in perfect equilibrium. Their connectivity is controlled through simple modelling operations of the mesh, which acts as a flexible membrane. This allows the calculation of the structural elements' distribution automatically from topological transformations while conserving the intuitive character of the software.

Fig. 19.2 Trans-Computational Pavilion 2.0. - 1:1 prototype created during the AA Visiting School Madrid 2014, directed by Manuel Jimenez. Exhibited during the XI Week of Architecture in Madrid at Roca Madrid Gallery. The pavilion is developed with flexible PVC pipes, assembled together to achieve local stiffness in the structure. Soft modelling is used as guidance for the assembly process. (Photography by Manuel Jimenez courtesy of bad design).
Design team: Manuel Jimenez Garcia, Roberto Garcia, Antonio Guijarro, Maria Olmos, Miguel A. Jimenez, Ignacio Viguera, Jorge Cerdá, Marina Rodriguez, Vicente Soler, Silvia Rivera, Maria Olmeda, Jose Real, Jose Luis E. Penelas.

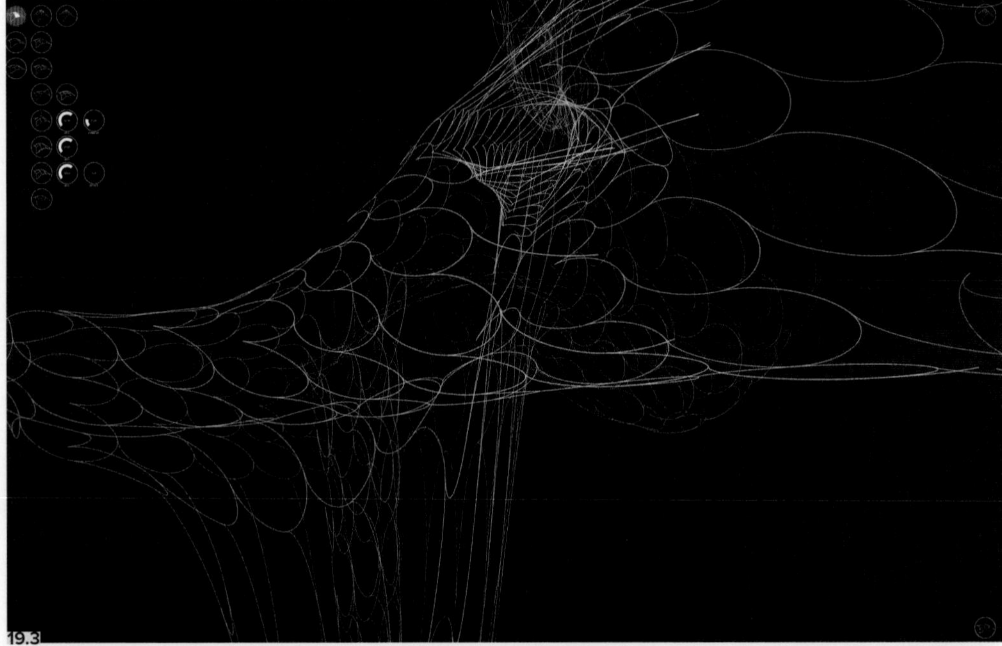

19.3

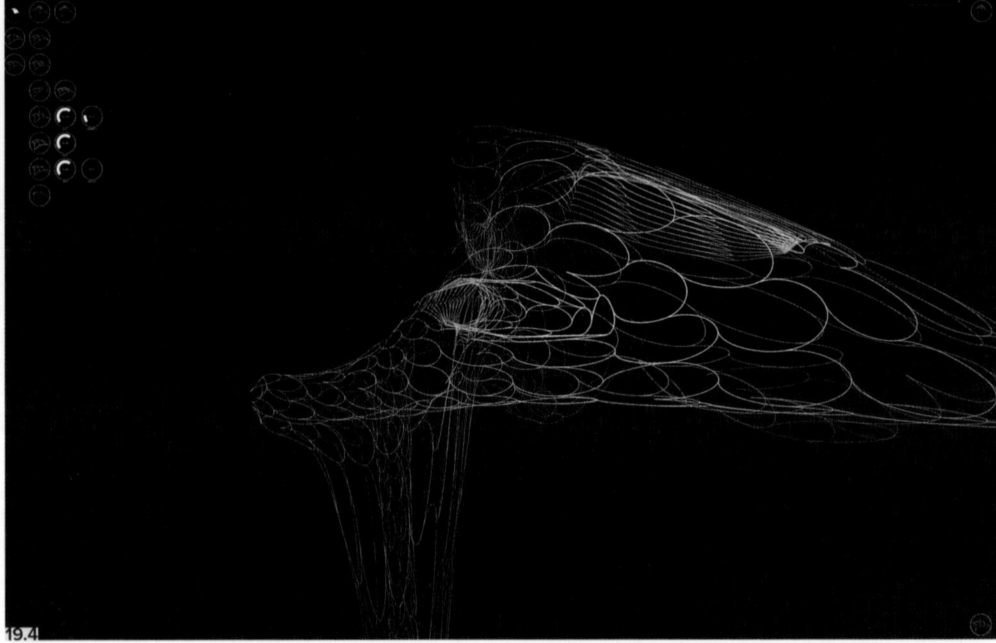

19.4

Fig. 19.3– 19.4 Screenshot of application in face selection mode, each face of the mesh is represented with the simulated spline, as a first step for the deployment of flexible material before construction. The local changes in the density of the structural elements are, at this stage, linked to the faces´subdivision. Soft modelling allows forecasting the behavior of the material, anticipating inflection points. The user develops a new intuitive approach towards material understanding.

Fig. 19.5 Vertices selection mode. In this mode, only particles position and state can be modified. The synchronization of particles – vertices/springs to edges – enables the constant updating of the positions of each part of the model.
There is constant feedback between the physical behavior of every particle-spring of the 3D mesh subdivision as well as the variable scale and depth at every point. This was developed using Toxiclibs by Karsten Schmidt as a physics library, and HEMesh by Frederik Vanhoutte for meshes.

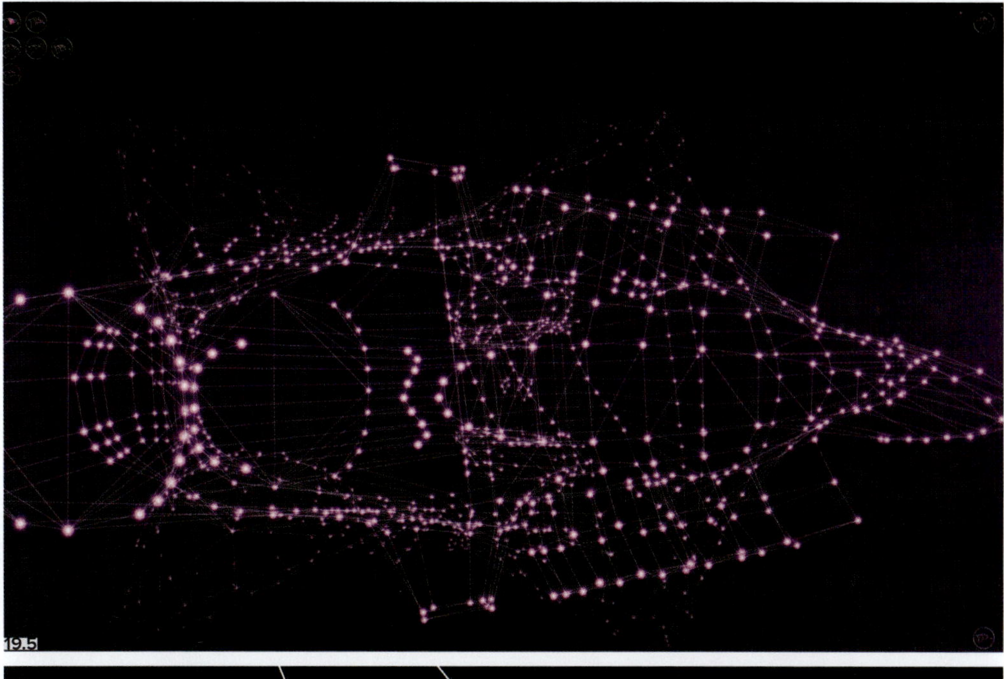
19.5

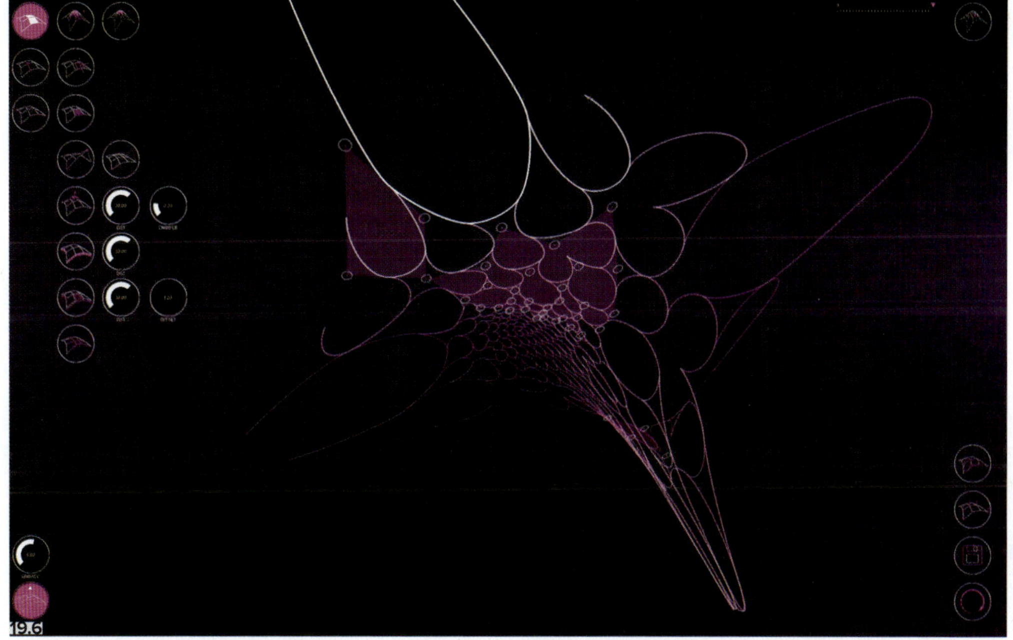
19.6

Fig. 19.6 Isolation of bezier piping structure. The link between discrete pieces and the mesh faces allows the creation of new workflows, in which designers can not only control a tensile structure with external anchor points and frames but also create the frame itself. Further development of the software aims to allow the discrete pieces to bend and connect following structural principles, linking the geometrical logic for their arrangement to stress values in the object.

Fig. 19.7 OffShore Bezier. - Installation produced during Dezact 2015 (Extra Fabrica) at Shin Chien University, Taipei. This 10 meters long structure is configured as an assemblage of bamboo pipes. The installation is hanged from three anchor points, distributed in different heights, up to 15 meters above the ground. Although SoftModelling was limited to an approximation in the structural arrangement, the software proved that the distribution and connectivity of discrete linear elements could be controlled real-time while in the modeling stage.
(Photography by Christina Dahdaleh courtesy of bad design).
Design team: Manuel Jimenez Garcia, Christina Dahdaleh, and Dezact students.

MANUEL JIMENEZ

SOCINEMATIC

F. MYLES SCIOTTO

F. Myles Sciotto is interested in the dynamics of space, sound and the dialogue between architecture and the body. He is currently a Ph.D Candidate at UCSB where his dissertation is on the generative methods between architecture and music. He received his Masters of Architecture from SCI-Arc where he received the Best Thesis Honor and holds a Lecturer position at USC School of Architecture teaching studios that focus on the role of sound and interactive real-time systems within the field of Architecture. More information can be found at his website soCinematic.com

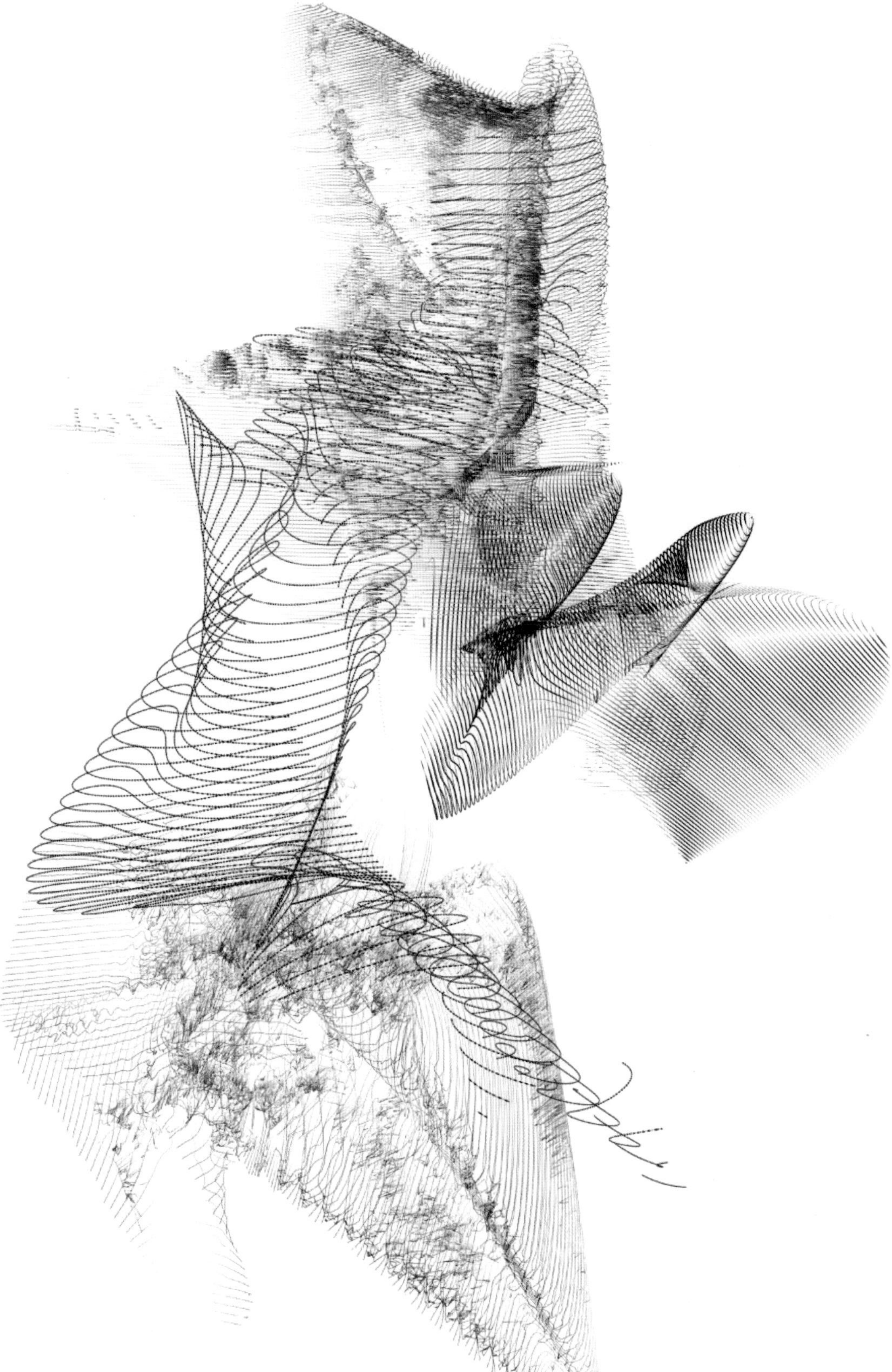

20.1

OTHERPLACES

How might one diagram the patterns found in a stream of collected data related to a certain experience? How would these patterns compare to the experience itself? How might these developments affect current fields of praxis and theory, might new fields merge or ideas that were once prevalent become relevant once again? How might these concepts materialize, generalize and perhaps most importantly, specialize? These are not new ideas; rather they are ideas that beg to be continually reimagined, reconstituted and reconfigured. Other-places and the ideas that led to its realization have their roots in these questions and point towards its relationship with architecture and spatial thinking.

These drawings do not follow a cognitive or neuro-scientific process, though they are produced by a methodical approach. They do not objectively define an emotion or feeling, though there may be a particular understanding to which the drawings allude. Technical processes are utilized without alienating our sensibility; the rule-based system subject to the rational nature of the intuitive, neither enslaved by the other. Sequences and structures grow from the micro to the macro, determining a compositional arrangement, a notational drawing, scoring one specific moment within a world, within each one of us, celebrating the local universal.

Other-Places are a series of six black and white drawings with an accompanying soundscape. The intention is to experience these two modalities together, focusing on hearing the drawings and seeing the sounds - the music of the mind. A Tope is a place, a specific and spatial moment chosen from a dynamical system unique to one person while connecting to the others, the Allo. Each drawing is unique and specific to each person and their experience. The work experimented with the selection of a moment from a continually evolving dynamic and near real-time system. A frozen moment is chosen using a balance between one's conscious taste, proportions of bio-data and the common patterns found throughout the others chosen moments.

Sensibility I Specificity =
Sense - Sample - Select - Scan - Synthesize

- The visual and aural translation of bio-data.
- Interacting with a self-generating system.
- Selecting a frozen moment from a dynamic system.
- Personal spatial preferences and proportions.
- Scanning for preferential patterns.
- Specification through the particular.

One at a time, six friends (three women and three men) were asked to sit in front of a large screen and a pair of speakers while wearing a wireless EEG headset that samples the electrical activity occurring in the brain. The content presented was a visual and aural composition that used the raw data from the EEG and translated it though variable spatial parameters, and into a scene of geometries, colors, textures, pitches, and intensities. This provided a window into a world where the user was witnessing an interpretation as it was occurring.

Immersed in their own continuously transforming experience, each friend was asked to select, freeze, and save a moment they found particularly compelling - a moment in the visual and aural space that they resonated with. Emphasis was placed on the decision by allowing the dynamic system to be frozen at any time giving the freedom to inspect and analyze the process, yet limiting the final selection

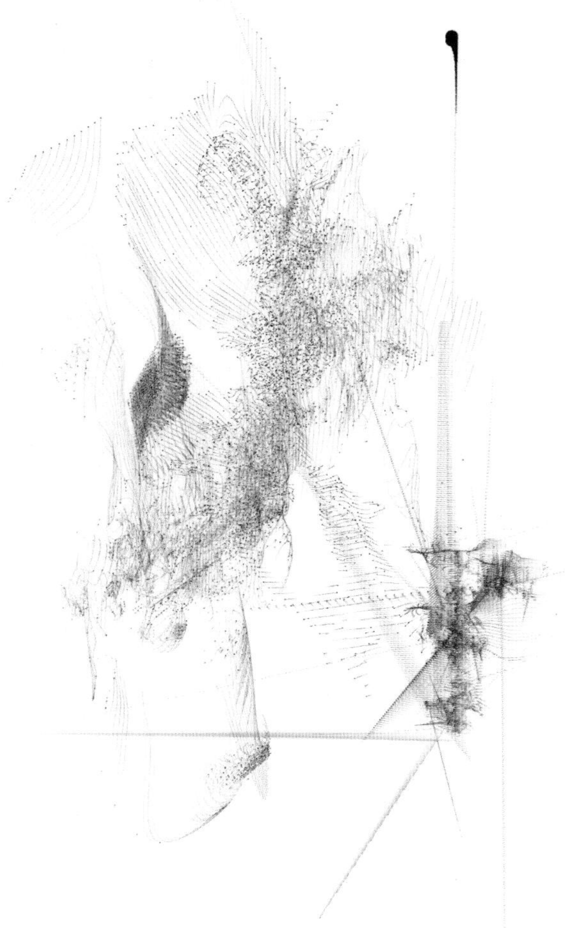

20.2

to only one moment. The data associated with this chosen moment was collected, saved, filtered and scanned, noting the proportions and patterns.

The results were compared across all sets, and a group-set was produced that fed-back into the weighting of the translation process, tuning each set to the common bond as a way to celebrating the different and the unity. This process finalized each chosen pattern and proportion was translated into geometry, and a final drawing of each person's space emerged. Lastly, a soundscape was composed using the resolved data, focused on translating the same proportions into temporal and harmonic cues. As each drawing exists in space and its corresponding sound is scored through time. One after another, each person's selection flows in and out as the group-set grounds the piece with its modulating flow and rhythm.

Project Resources:
Allotopes Soundscape:
soundcloud.com/socinematic/allotopes-blindspot
Allotopes Website:
http://alternity.info/works/allotopes/

Special Thanks:
Daniel Berlin, Jean-Michel Crettaz, Carl Krull, Erin Lani, Marcos Novak, Rafael Sampaio Rocha, Micheal Rotondi, Somewhere Something, Julie Valentin

20.3

Fig. 20.1 -20.3 Tope number 1
Tope number 2
Tope number 3

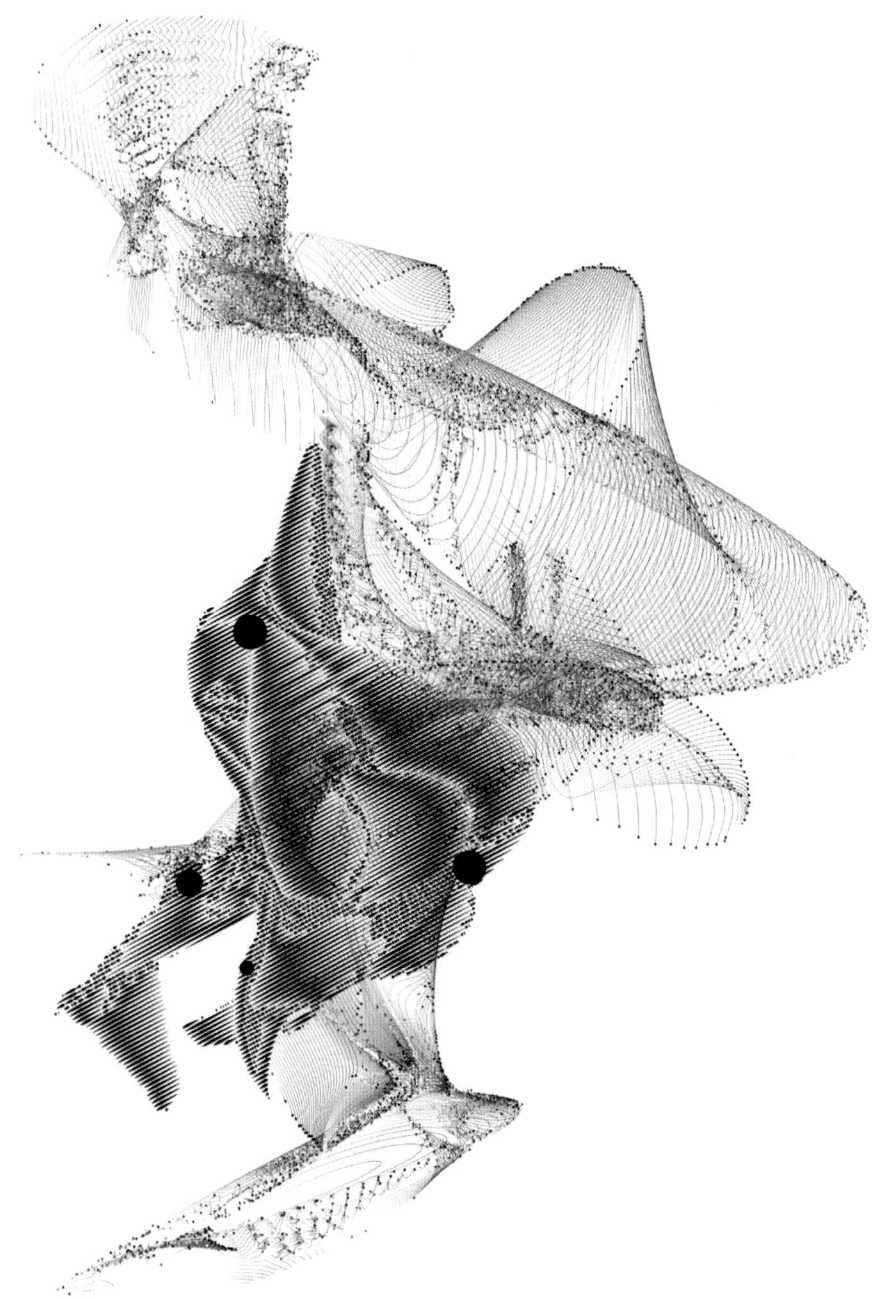

20.4

Fig. 20.4 Tope number 4

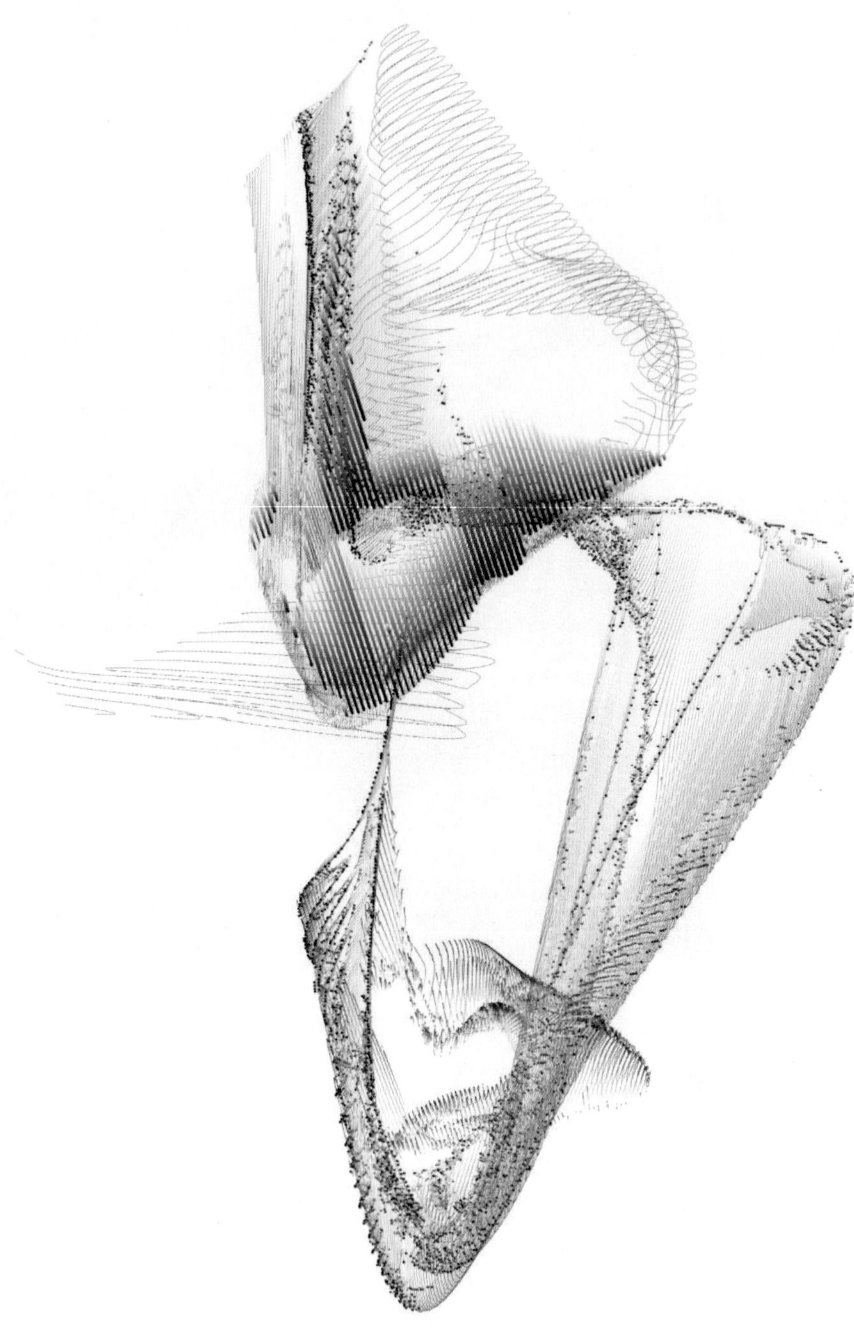

20.5

Fig. 20.5 Tope number 5

20.6

Fig. 20.6 Tope number 6

ROBOTICS / INTERACTIVE DESIGN

JASON KELLY JOHNSON

Jason Kelly Johnson is a founding design partner of Future Cities Lab, an experimental design and research office based in San Francisco, California. Working in collaboration with his partner Nataly Gattegno, Jason has produced a range of award-winning projects exploring the intersections of design with advanced fabrication technologies, robotics, responsive building systems and public space. Future Cities Lab is at the forefront of exploring how advanced technologies, social media and the internet of things will profoundly affect how we live, work, communicate and play in the future. Their approach to design and making, which has been described as "high-performance craft", is also deeply experiential, interactive and materially rich. Future Cities Lab is an interdisciplinary studio employing an adventurous team of designers, architects, technologists, digital craftspeople, urban ecologists and more. Jason is also a tenured Associate Professor at the California College of the Arts (CCA) in San Francisco and co-directs CCA's Digital Craft Lab. He has also recently taught at Cornell University, UVa and UPenn, and UC Berkeley.

ARCHITECTURE AND THE SINGULARITY: EMERGING PROTOCOLS FOR DESIGN

The Singularity refers to a hypothetical moment in the not-so-distant future when there will be a merging of humans and machines, where non-biological intelligence will evolve and ultimately surpass us. As the computer scientist and futurist Ray Kurzweil has noted, “The result will be an intimate merger between the technology-creating species and the technological evolutionary process it spawned. We’ll get to a point where technical progress will be so fast that unenhanced human intelligence will be unable to follow it. That will mark the Singularity.”

In 2012, Kurzweil was employed full-time by Google to explore these ideas in the context of their radically expanding corporate portfolio. By early 2015 Google had acquired a cluster of the world’s most cutting-edge companies in the fields of machine learning, artificial intelligence, and robotics including Industrial Perception, Meka Robotics, Boston Dynamics, Bot & Dolly, Redwood Robotics and DeepMind Technologies. They also incubated companies focused on smart cities such as Waze, Sidewalk Labs, and the Driverless Car Project, and companies operating at the edges of architecture and the so-called “internet of things” like Flux Factory and Nest. When added to their already robust products like Google Search, Analytics and Maps, the company’s vast holdings have set the stage for a radical entanglement with the future of the physical environment. In the future, it is increasingly becoming clear that the singularity will profoundly affect how we live, work, play and engage with everything from fashion, furniture, art, architecture and public space.

The field of architecture, including the advanced technological processes the discipline routinely employs - from simulation to design to fabrication and construction - will very likely be at the forefront of working with, or perhaps proving resistance to these entanglements. If we are to follow Kurzweil’s hypothesis, the speculative narrative as it concerns architecture might go something like this: In the first phase, as we can already see happening today, architects are employing low-level machines to complete their work more precisely and more efficiently. For example they regularly utilize machines to precisely scan building sites, or use algorithms to guide design and fabrication processes. Nevertheless, humans are still more or less “in charge”. In the second phase, as the use of artificially intelligent autonomous vehicles becomes safe and widespread in the transportation sector, the architecture, engineering and construction industries will eagerly embrace allied technologies and methods. These industries will willingly adopt the use of autonomous machines with superhuman intelligence to guide them through all aspects of the design to construction processes. In this phase the architect’s disciplinary knowledge, in all its richness and complexity, will be replicated by machines but not necessarily surpassed by it. In the third phase, Kurzweil predicts that the capacity for machines to evolve knowledge and skillsets superior to our own will inevitably occur. The world will enter a phase of “singularity” where networked intelligent machines will scan, design, build and rebuild the world as they see fit, and not necessarily with direct human input, guidance or interaction. These robotic ecologies will operate in an evolutionary fashion without the restraints of human physiology, intelligence or historical reference.

It is with this narrative in mind that we can

understand and appreciate much of the explorations detailed in this chapter of the publication. The projects outlined here all reference possible futures where machine learning, artificial intelligence, and robotics - cornerstones of the singularity - are paramount to architecture, fabrication and interaction.

Sensing, planning, acting, and feedback: These are the emerging protocols for a new class of networked architecture that is progressively exhibiting behavioral, heuristic and evolutionary capacities. It is well documented that A.I. (artificial intelligence) is quietly being woven into the digital and physical fabric of everyday life including our bodies, gadgets, games, buildings, landscapes, and cities. Its reach is increasingly prolific and surreptitious. Not only is this shifting how we are communicating and interacting with the world, but it is profoundly changing how we are thinking, designing, making and sharing. As such, the design research included in this publication highlights a growing body of experimental work by architects and designers focused on exploring the creative, conceptual and technical possibilities of these emerging protocols. While attributed to predominantly technical disciplines, they suggest that the domain of emerging creative practices will increasingly cross-over into allied experimental fields like computer science, robotics, engineering and interaction design.

Some might argue that these protocols merely apply or build upon technological insights shared by Vitruvius in his De Architectura treatise over 500 hundred years ago: the importance of engineering creative machines, the manufacturing of custom materials, and the invention of instruments to survey and map the world. In many ways the work in this publication suggests something more profound: it forecasts a world where knowledge is not only shared or exchanged, but is accelerated and intensified by feedback loops and open source networks of designers, programmers, machinists, material scientists, and the like. The emerging protocols of architecture and the singularity suggest a coming world where the matter at all scales is evolutionary and potentially programmable, parametric, kinetic and intermeshed with artificial intelligence.

The contributions collected here forecast a fundamental change - where architecture and artificial intelligence begin to productively coexist and coevolve. By coupling this change with the ubiquity of embedded computation, networked technologies, and open-source resources, tomorrow's designers will be able to explore, design and construct interactive prototypes that have in the past remained unfeasible due to their cost and complexity. By experimenting across scales, for instance linking sensor-laden physical models to much larger and complex simulations, the potential impact of these methodologies on architecture and urban scale explorations holds immense promise. As these prototypes get hybridized and integrated with responsive technologies, they will have the capacity to better process and respond to the variable and multi-scalar inputs from their environments. In-situ sensing inputs and cybernetic capacities are now possible mediums to be experimentally mined for their experiential, spatial, material and ecological potentials.

These tangible data-informed prototypes can create visceral, immersive and participatory human experiences. In the past, to allow for the sheer collection and processing of large datasets, inputs were limited to just a few select parameters. With our increased capabilities to compute large amounts of information the virtualization and networking of the physical world also open up the opportunity for communication and real-time feedback with systems like social networks and the internet of things. At the scale of the city, one could argue that 'feedback' has typically been explored as a linear relationship between a human and its built environment: data accumulated over long periods of time about social and biological processes, and a more or less static physical context. What are the implications when these sensing, planning, acting and feedback loops are real-time when contextual data is live, and our algorithms allow us to evolve life-like characteristics and intelligence-laden ecologies?

While the opportunities to explore these protocols and methodologies are enormous, they are still in their early stages. The work collected here, while provocative and extraordinary, stimulates more questions than it answers. How will these protocols transform the way we approach the design of architecture in the future? How will we embed feedback loops, encode and network our buildings and cities? How can we leverage these protocols to address mounting social, political and ecological issues? Perhaps most challenging, as the so-called singularity approaches, what pedagogical approaches will the design disciplines need to adopt to explore and engage these protocols to their fullest extent?

BEHNAZ FARAHI

Behnaz Farahi is a designer, architect, and Annenberg Fellow at the USC School of Cinematic Arts. She is interested in interactive environments and their relationship to the human body. In particular, she is interested in the integrated application of material performance, and smart materials in contemporary art/architecture practice. Behnaz Farahi has an Undergraduate and two Masters degrees in Architecture and is now a Ph.D. candidate in the Media Arts and Practices program at USC.

Behnaz Farahi has also worked with Professor Behrokh Khoshnevis on a NASA funded research project developing a robot to print structures on the Moon.

Her work has been widely published and exhibited. It has been selected for Skyline2014 in Downtown Los Angeles, ACADIA 2013 conference in Canada, 'Sight+ Sound+ Space' iMAP exhibition in 2013, 'Design Intelligence: Advanced Computational Research' exhibition in Beijing in 2013, the 'Encoding Architecture' exhibition in Carnegie Mellon University in 2013. In 2013 she was awarded the first prize for the Kinetic Art Organization international competition.

Blindspot Initiati

ROBOTIC 3D PRINTED BODY ARCHITECTURE

3D printing and interactive design have revolutionized approaches to design in many different industries, including fashion and wearable and architectural design.
Advances in 3D printing technologies have enabled us to design shape shifting objects, by carefully designing materials in various compositions and forms, so as to open up a variety of mechanical behaviors. This provides us with the opportunity to design objects that are becoming closer to natural systems in terms of their morphologies as well as their behaviors.
Moreover, advances in interactive design technologies are changing the way that we interact with the world around us by influencing our perception, ways of communication, and awareness. Thanks to embedded computing and biometric sensors, our bodies can now operate as primarily interactive interfaces with the world, through the use of interactive systems.
By describing the design process behind two projects, Bodyscape and Caress of the Gaze, this paper aims to illustrate a new approach to the design of robotic 3D printed body architecture.

Bodyscape

Bodyscape is an interactive 3D printed fashion item inspired by the skin of the human body. It lights up as the wearer moves, raising fashion to a higher level, as the poetic dance of light and human movement.

The aim here is twofold: firstly, Bodyscape is an attempt to explore the role of geometry in creating a dynamic 3D printed structure for the world of fashion. And, secondly, it is an attempt to create an interactive lighting system so as to amplify the performative qualities of human bodily movement, and to create an enchanting illuminated choreography of the body.

3D printing technologies are developing rapidly, and it is now possible to print using soft materials, but such technologies are not available all the time. Most 3D printers still use rigid materials. How then might we reconfigure the design of a fashion item that is 3D printed using rigid materials so that it bends and flexes as though it were made of soft materials? New research shows that the crucial aspect of the behavior of 3D printed materials is their geometrical configuration. Spirals, springs and curvilinear forms have greater inherent flexibility. Bodyscape draws upon these principles to create a dynamic, flexible outfit despite being printed by using rigid, fragile materials.

A further strategy was to engage with the behavior and physical properties of the human skin. Bodyscape is based on the Langer lines of the skin. Langer lines are the topological lines of skin tension, discovered initially in 1861 by the anatomist, Karl Langer. These are the lines of least tension that correspond to the natural orientation of collagen fibers in the dermis of the skin, which are generally parallel to the orientation of the underlying muscle fibers. For this reason surgeons use them to determine where to cut the skin during an operation especially in the case of cosmetic surgery. Most surgeons prefer to make an incision parallel to the Langer lines so that the skin can heal better afterwards as there is minimum tension between these lines. Bodyspace therefore uses both the principles of the spiral as a naturally flexible form and the logic of Langer lines to produce a flexible garment that moves in harmony with the human body.

Finally, interactive lighting systems have been integrated beneath the surface in order to enhance the dynamic performativity of the wearer's movement. A small gyroscope capable of detecting and tracking the 9

21.2

axis shoulder movements of the wearer sends data to a small microcontroller that illuminates two addressable LED strips placed beneath the surface. As a result various lighting patterns emerge according to the forces being exerted by the body as it dances its way through space.

Caress of the Gaze

Caress of the Gaze is an interactive multi material 3D-printed garment, which can detect other people's gaze and respond accordingly with a life-like behavior.

Our skin is constantly in motion. It expands, contracts and changes its shape based on various internal and external stimuli including not only temperature and moisture but also feelings such as fear, excitement and anger. But what if our clothing could itself behave as an artificial 'skin' capable of changing its shape and operating as an interface with the world, so as to express various social issues such as intimacy, gender and personal identities?

This project offers a vision of the future by exploring the possibility of a second skin fabricated using multi-material 3D printing. The project demonstrates how the very latest and most advanced 3D printing technologies might contribute to the realm of fashion, by exploring the tectonic properties of the materials printed using an Objet500 Connex 3D printer. This technology allows the fabrication of composite materials with varying flexibilities, densities, and can combine materials in several ways with different material properties, all deposited in a single print run. Inspired by the flexible behavior of the reptile skin, Caress of the Gaze exhibits different behaviors over different parts of the body ranging from rigid to flexible.

For the design of Caress of the Gaze, a cellular mesh, which can hold scale-like members, has been used. The cellular mesh is able to provide sufficient flexibility to afford a range of desirable dynamic behaviors such as twisting, flexing and bending. The cellular mesh also controls the position of the scales, their overlap and hence also their interactions. Meanwhile, the size of the scales and their respective flexibility/rigidity is also essential to control

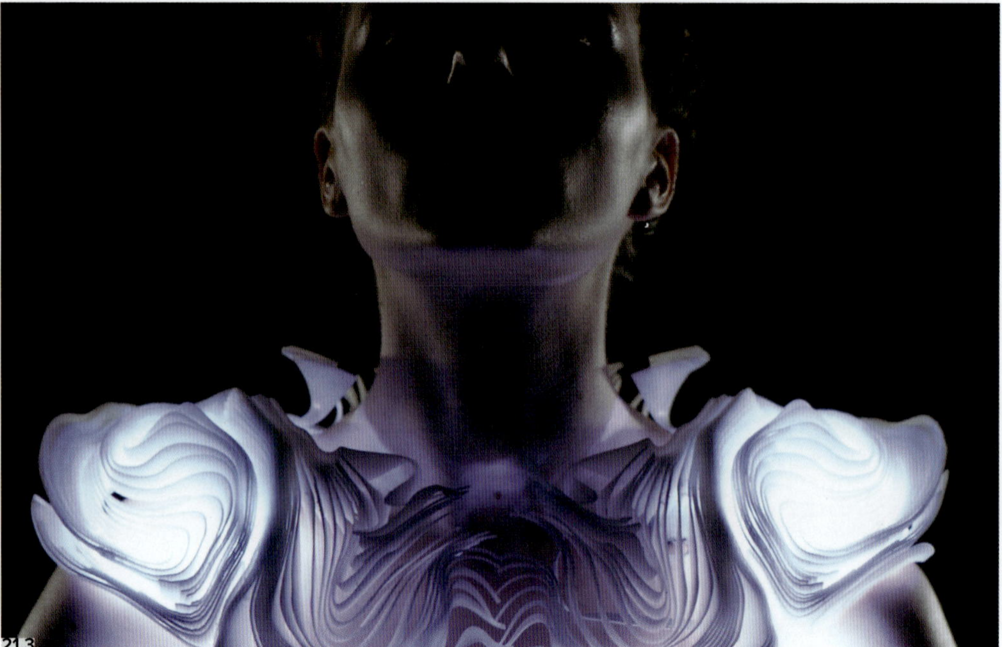

Fig. 21.1 Bodyscape by Behnaz Farahi, 3D printed interactive fashion item responding to the wearer's movement. Photo by Kyle Smithers, 2017.

Fig. 21.2 Close up of Bodyscape, Photo by Kyle Smithers, 2017.

Fig. 21.3 Bodyscape equipped with 9-axis a gyroscope and a small microcontroller controlling the lighting pattern of two LED strips mounted underneath the structure. Photo by Kyle Smithers, 2017.

the distribution of forces as well as to give the garment a certain aesthetic expression. A series of experiments were therefore conducted to explore the different ratios of soft and flexible to stiff materials on the scale-like members. While the flexible material (Shore 60 Black in this case) provides flexibility to the entire structure, the rigid material (Vero White in this case) provides structural rigidity. The lessons from these experiments were then applied to the form of the garment, so as to allow it to move, bristle and change its shape based on stimuli from the onlooker's gaze.

The project also explores the potential of an actuation system, assembled as a form of muscle system using Shape Memory Alloy actuators (SMA) that informs the motion of the artificial 'skin'.

Finally, Caress of the Gaze also investigates how our clothing might interact with other people as a primary interface. For this purpose an image sensing camera with a lens of less than 3mm, and capable of detecting the gender, age and orientation of the gaze of an onlooker, is positioned underneath the garment's quills. This data is relayed to a Teensy microcontroller on the back of the garment, that actuates and controls a network of Shape Memory Alloy wires that control the behavior of the garment, so that it responds to the onlooker's gaze.

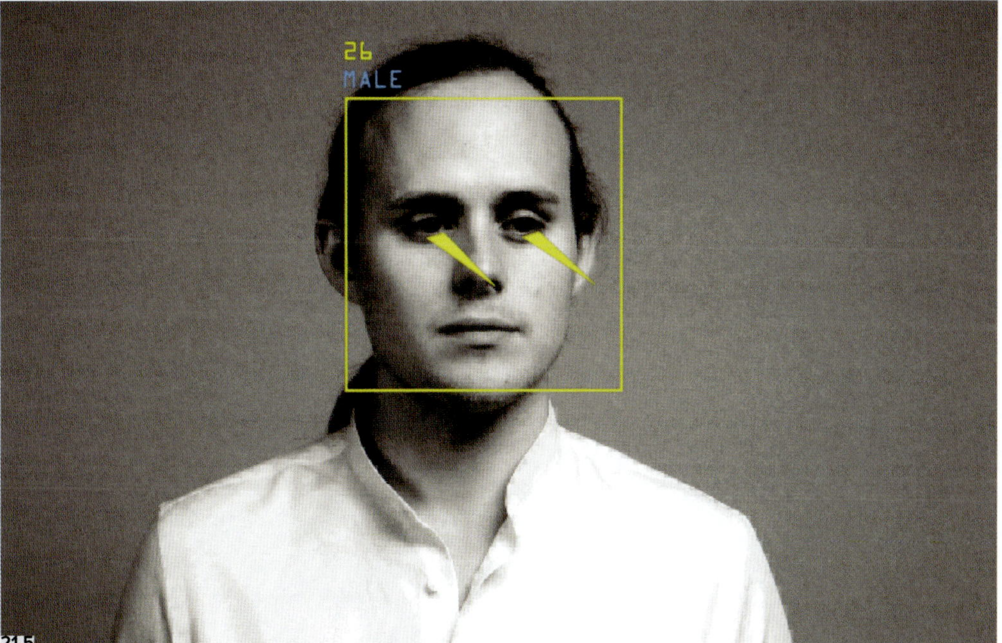

Fig. 21.4 Small tracking camera -with lens smaller than 3mm embedded underneath the quills. Photo by Charlie Nordstrom, 2015.

Fig. 21.5 Caress of the Gaze equipped with facial tracking camera, detecting age, gender and gaze orientation of the onlookers. Photo by Charlie Nordstrom, 2015.

Fig. 21.6-21.7 Caress of the Gaze by Behnaz Farahi, 3D printed gaze-actuated garment responding to the onlookers' gaze. Photo by Elena Kulikova, 2015.

BOTLAB

ZACH SCHOCH

Zachary Schoch is a Roboticist, Inventor, Designer, and founder of Bot Laboratory.

Through a careful fusion of his diverse backgrounds in mechanical engineering, race car design, and architecture (Master of Architecture from SCI-ARC), Zach has designed and developed the Euclid Robot 3D printer, a large scale Cartesian machine, and the RON 2.1 Extruder, a pellet fed plastics extruder. By using these two machines, Zach can design and print elements at spatial and architectural scale. Through exploring the potential of machines and their impact on architecture, Zach seeks to revolutionize the way we create and build space. Aside from Bot Laboratory, Zach also teaches and helps out at institutional environments such as Woodbury University and the University of Southern California.

BOTLAB

BotLaboratory has spent the past three years researching large-scale 3d printing. The challenge has been to print quickly, affordably, but also precisely. To meet the given criteria,

BotLaboratory takes on a more holistic approach to 3d printing. From machining parts to scripting and even electrical wiring, BotLaboratory chooses to do everything "in-house".

BotLaboratory's research can be categorized into two fields; fabrication (real-world // physical) and control (digital // simulation). While the two can be seen as disparate entities, by considering he two as an intertwined system, BotLaboratory seeks to use the robot as a flexible design tool to move it beyond the current pedestrian use as a mere tool for completing tasks.

On the fabrication front of BotLaboratory, the two key components are the Euclid Bot and the RON extruder. The former is a Cartesian gantry that moves in the XYZ coordinate planes and the latter is the extruder head which can handle a variety of plastics.

The control of the robots is done through a simulation environment known as Grasshopper.

Grasshopper allows for real-time and mostly error-free control of the robots in both virtual and physical space. The existing digital set-up creates a safe environment to design and experiment in. All designs are first tested in virtual space and, due to the inherent nature of digital tools, can be easily printed in real-time.

Developing bespoke tools, BotLaboratory can control the material and detailing in the manufacturing process, effectively going from digital file to factory. BotLaboratory has even found innovative ways to break the norms in 3D printing through non-vertical contouring,

printing without support, and printing on other prints.

The development of the BotLaboratory machines are still in progress. Pushing the limits of the available tools and technology, while developing the tools that will allow the robots to interface with materials and the environment will continue to be integral to BotLaboratory. These tools are no less than the devices that enable a robotic system to do work and will be developed in a coordinated fashion with future research endeavors.

For the Blindspot exhibition, BotLaboratory showcased a series of 3d printed objects, which encapsulate the manufacturing process through material properties.

22.1

Fig.22.1 6' 4" (1.9 meters) 3D printed wall created for Maker Faire 2014. Printed on the Euclid Robot 3D printer using both black and clear ABS plastic it is extremely strong with an approximately 1/4" (6.35mm) print thickness.The wall is two 5 hour prints making for 10 hours of total print time. And yes, that is fast, well compared to most printers.

22.2

Fig. 22.2 Designed and constructed from the ground up the Euclid robot 3d printer is a cartesian 3-axis 3D printer with a 1.1*1.1*1.1 meter build volume. Utilizing custom Grasshopper path planning software allowing unique printing techniques including non-planar print layers and non-regular print thickness.

Fig. 22.3 Printing in mid-air with no support whatsoever using polystyrene.Additional nozzle cooling was utilized as well as very reduced movement speed. The left image is simple a two vertical lines con- nected by a diagonal.The verticals are very good however the diagonal has some droop. Right is a cylindri-cal spiral (constant radius).The noticeably uneven result is believed to be caused by having cooling that is relative to the axis of the extruder radially uneven. To counteract this, a donut-like air nozzle was con- structed but has yet to be tested.

Fig. 22.4 Detail view of s-wall connection.This detail was designed to have a tension element on the outside of the building (hook and match- ing receptacle left center) and a compression element on the inside.The joint is simply disconnected by reversing the load path.

Fig. 22.5 Because the tension element (outer seam) is placed below the com- pression element (inner seam) the snap connection should prevent any water intrusion. Additionally, a sealing gasket could be integrated into the connection to prevent vapor and air intrusion.

22.6

Fig. 22.6 Modular 3D printed full-scale building system featuring large high strength ABS components that structurally snap together allowing for easy transport and assembly by hand.Total print time for these three pieces was less than 18 hours. Assistance with printing and 3d modeling for s-wall from Eugene Lee.

Because these components are built from such high-performance material they should be constructible by hand, or for larger and more structurally elements only minimal equipment would be required.This property allows for investment in higher performance printing facilities due to the low cost of transportation to the build- ing site.

With this construction system, there is no fundamental difference between the traditionally disparate elements of floor/wall/roof. In this instance, the floor becomes the wall, and the wall becomes the roof/ceiling.

Fig.22.7 The Euclid 3d printer. Note the steel print bed has an o.s.b. spoil board. The bright orange loop seen on the side of the extruder is the cooling air that is fed from the off-board compressor through the center of the Z-axis tube.

22.7

ZACH SCHOCH

Blindspot Initiative

RUAIRI GLYNN

Artist Ruairi Glynn is set to install a dramatic new robotic installation entitled 'Fearful Symmetry' in the Tanks at Tate Modern on 21-22 August 2012. Specially commissioned for the Tate's Undercurrent programme, the installation promises to provide a unique visceral and memorable experience which will encourage visitors to see the Tanks in a new light.

Glynn is known for interactive kinetic works that reveal the primacy of movement above and beyond color, form, and texture in human visual perception. His work draws on a rich heritage of cybernetics, puppetry, and dance to achieve this.

FEARFUL SYMMETRY

Within the subterranean bowels of The Tanks, something primitive animates the darkness of Tate Modern's dramatic new gallery space.

A glowing tetrahedron glides through the air, suspended above peoples heads from a 21-meter motorized rail holding the world's largest delta robot. As the only light source in the room, the tetrahedron acts as entertainer and guide to space, dancing with the audience, and playfully encouraging them to become an active part of the performance. Through the interplay of luminous form and motion, ambiguity in visual perception is explored and manipulated in an unfolding interactive performance between the public and a kinetic installation.

"This work is a direct reaction to The Tanks space itself," says Glynn. "We will fill the space with the sounds of this living machine, mixed live by our team of sound artists. The movements have been choreographed by master puppeteers with a lifetimes' experience breathing life into inanimate objects. The entire installation will constantly be creating a different environment from one moment to the next, and is completely reactive to the audience in the space."

The work builds on Glynn's earlier pieces, Motive Colloquies (2011, Pompidou Centre Paris) and Performative Ecologies (2008, National Art Museum Beijing). Both of these examined the way in which audiences react to differing roboticised dances - but this is his most ambitious project to date. Taking its title from William Blake's "The Tyger", the installation returns visitors to a primal state of hyper-awareness through advanced computer vision, robotics and interactive choreography, the sum of which creates an intense, visceral and primal way to experience the Tate's Tanks.

The work is part of the Tate's Undercurrent programme directed at young audiences through a series of events, installations, and interventions by audio, visual and performance artists.

Glynn describes how "the installation engages with a treasure of a youthful mind, the ability to wilfully suspend disbelief, often a faculty lost slowly and imperceptibly with age. Young audiences of my installations care little for the technology that animates the work. So ever-present in their lives, they take it for granted, focusing instead much more on experience. They, in this respect, are my greatest critics. Equally, they are my greatest allies in their wilful suspension of disbelief at the perceptual boundaries between analog and digital, creature and machine, life and death."

Release yourself from civilized thought, suspend your disbelief and play, perform and explore the Tanks with Fearful Symmetry.

23.1

Fig. 23.1 Precise motion control of the delta robot manipulator was critical, but far more important was creating the perception that the movements were purposeful. With sophisticated analysis of the publics gestures, the autonomous robot reciprocated with perceptible intelligence and emotion.

23.3

Fig. 23.2 The cavernous concrete chamber of the south tank, 32m in diameter, 7m tall, had previously lain dormant for decades cloaked in darkness. The response to the site – a living luminaire revealing the dramatic space as it moved around the gallery interacting with the visiting public. Primitive in appearance, to avoid figuratively inferring life, a piercing glowing tetrahedron, glided through the air, swooping down to play with visitors and fleeing up and away if too many got close.

Fig. 23.3 Encouraging the public to suspend their disbelief and play with the living luminaire, the more people engaged gesturally with the work, the more enthusiastic its responses would be.

Fig. 23.4-23.6 Hidden up above in the darkness, like a long string marionette puppeteer, a 5m tall autonomous Delta Robot, custom built to manipulate the motion of the luminaire beneath it, moved back and forth through the space on a 21-meter motorized rail. An array of Kinect Sensors mounted on the traveling robot built a real-time 3D point cloud of its local environment, detecting the public, and reading their movements using gesture recognition algorithms. Reciprocally the agile performer responded with behaviors choreographed with the collaboration of a team of puppeteers giving the machine its uncannily human character.

23.6